# PRESBYTERIANS AND THE REVOLUTION

# PRESBYTERIANS
## AND
# THE REVOLUTION

BY THE

REV. W. P. BREED, D.D.

---



---

**AMERICAN VISION PRESS**

POWDER SPRINGS, GEORGIA

PRESBYTERIANS AND THE REVOLUTION



First Published in 1876.



Printed in the United States.

*Typesetting by Amy Vallorani*
*Layout design by Adam Stiles and Luis Lovelace*
*Cover design by Luis Lovelace*

**American Vision, Inc.**
3150 Florence Road, Suite 2
Powder Springs, Georgia 30127-5385

www.AmericanVision.org
1-800-628-9460

ISBN 10: 0-915815-30-3
ISBN 13: 978-0-915815-30-2

# Table of Contents

Chapter 1
**Presbyterians and the Centennial** . . . . . . . . . . . . . . . . . . . . 9

Chapter 2
**Presbyterianism:** *A Representative Republican Form of Government* . . . . . . . . . . . . . . . . . . . . . . . . . . . . . 19

Chapter 3
**Presbyterianism:** *Odious to Tyrants* . . . . . . . . . . . . . . . . . . . . . . . . . . . . . . . . . . . . . . . . 27

Chapter 4
**Presbyterian Spirit In Harmony With That of the Revolution** . . . . . . . . . . . . . . . . . . . . . . . . 33

Chapter 5
**The Westmoreland County Resolutions** . . . . . . . . . . . . . . . . . . . . . . . . . . . . . . . . . . 43

Chapter 6
**The Mecklenburg Declaration** . . . . . . . . . . . . . . . . . . . . . . . . 49

Chapter 7
**Presbyterian Zeal and Suffering** . . . . . . . . . . . . . . . . . . . . . 59

Chapter 8
**Formal Action of the Presbyterian Church** . . . . . . . . . . . . . . . . . . . . . . . . . . . . . . 75

Chapter 9
**Declaration of Independence and Dr. John Witherspoon** ............................. 91

Chapter 10
**Organization of the Confederacy** .................... 109

Chapter 11
**Monument to Witherspoon** ............................ 117

# 1

# Presbyterians and the Centennial

It was to be expected that the approach of the one hundredth anniversary of our nation's birth would awaken a profound interest in the public mind and give rise to measures for a commemorative recognition in some degree befitting the occasion.

Of necessity the national thought reverts to those stirring times that so grandly tried the souls of men and issued in the creation of this gigantic republic. Again on our eye flashes the light of those guns that laid the martyrs low on Lexington Green and at Concord Bridge. Again to our ear comes the report of "the shot heard round the world." The heroic devotion of those men, who, for the sake of a principle, so calmly offered their breasts to the deadly leaden hail, stirs with a fresh impulse the patriotic virtues within us and lifts our manhood higher in our esteem. Anew there passes across the field of our vision that grand procession of sages and statesmen and military heroes, and we thank the God of nations for a generation of men so fitted for the exigencies of such a day and hour.

History has abundantly verified the insight of Chatham as displayed in his fervid eloquence in the House of Lords, in January, 1775:

"When your lordships look at the papers transmitted us from America, when you consider their decency, firmness and wisdom, you cannot but respect their cause and wish to make it your own.

"For myself I must avow that in all my reading—and I have read Thucydides and have studied and admired the master-states of the world—for solidity of reason, force of sagacity and wisdom of conclusion under a complication of difficult circumstances, no nation or body of men can stand in preference to the general congress at Philadelphia. The histories of Greece and Rome give us nothing to equal to it."

The bustle also of the town meeting breaks on the ear. We hear the broad-browed yeomen discussing the foundation principles of free government and closing the discussion with the high resolve for liberty or death. The provincial congress gathers and thrills with the burning sentences that spring from the lips of an Adams or a Patrick Henry. The Continental Congress assembles, doubtful of its powers, uncertain as to what wisdom demands, hindered by countless obstacles, only one thing clear, and that is their inflexible determination not to submit to the tyrannies of the British king and his parliament. For a time apparent, chaos reigns; but through all the will of God is working toward order and organization, and the result is, first, victory in the field, second, a confederacy of the colonies, and third, that wonderful embodiment of human ability and ripe statesmanship, the national Constitution.

"The structure," says Judge Story, "has been erected by architects of consummate skill and fidelity. Its foundations are solid; its compartments beautiful as well as useful; its arrangements are full of wisdom and order, and its defences are impregnable from without.

"In the sunshine of peace and in the storm of war the Constitution of the United States of America has had a severe but impartial trial. It has amply fulfilled the expectation of its friends and completely dissipated the fears of its early opponents.

"As a great rule of political conduct it has guided the country, through unprecedented political vicissitudes and perilous

In the sunshine of peace and in the storm of war the Constitution of the United States of America has had a severe but impartial trial. It has amply fulfilled the expectation of its friends and completely dissipated the fears of its early opponents.

Joseph Story

revolutionary commotions among the nations, to a condition at once so prosperous and commanding that it has wholly outstripped all foresight and calculation.

"When we look at the vast theatre on which, under the influence of its provisions, our maritime trade has been employed, the freedom and prosperity we enjoy at home, the respect entertained for our country abroad, our thankfulness to God ought to know no bounds."

In his oration at the late centennial celebration at Concord, Mr. George William Curtis well said:

> At the end of a century we can see the work of this day as our fathers could not; we can see that then the final movement began of a process long and unconsciously preparing, which was to entrust liberty to new forms, and institutions that seemed full of happy promise for mankind. And now for nearly a century what was formerly called the experiment

of a representative republic of imperial extent and power has been tried. Has it fulfilled the hopes of its founders and the just expectations of mankind? I have already glanced at its early and fortunate conditions, and we know how vast and splendid [was] its early growth and development. Our material statistics soon dazzled the world. Europe no longer sneered, but gazed in wonder, waiting and watching. Our population doubled every fifteen years, and our wealth every ten years. Every little stream among the hills turned a mill; and the great inland seas, bound by the genius of Clinton to the ocean, became the highway of boundless commerce, the path of unprecedented empire. Our farms were the granary of other lands. Our cotton-fields made England rich. Still, we chased the whale in the Pacific Ocean and took fish in the tumbling seas of Labrador. We hung our friendly lights along thousands of miles of coast to tempt the trade of every clime; and wherever, on the dim rim of the globe there was a harbor, it was white with American sails. Meanwhile, at home, the political foreboding of Federalism had died away, and its very wail seemed a tribute to the pacific glories of the land.

*The ornament of beauty is suspect,*
*A crow that flies in heaven's sweetest air.*

The government was felt to be but a hand of protection and blessing; labor was fully employed; capital was secured; the army was a jest; enterprise was pushing through the Alleghanies, grasping and settling the El Dorado of the prairies, and still, having

> traversed the wilderness, reached out toward the Rocky Mountains, and reversing the voyage of Columbus, rediscovered the Old World from the New.

With a career behind us such as this, and with such scenes of prosperity around us, it was impossible that the hundredth anniversary of the nation's birth should be allowed to pass without some marked recognition of the event, at least on the part of the city where our independence was born and our government brought into being.

It is now certain that the year 1876 will see hundreds of thousands of our own nation, and crowds from other nations, of every kindred, tribe and tongue, thronging the city of Philadelphia to take part in a succession of exciting services commemorative of the time when our fathers, under the inspiration of principles derived from God's holy word, at the ringing of that bell that proclaimed "liberty throughout all the land, unto all the inhabitants thereof," and chanting as they marched, "All men are created equal, and are endowed by their Creator with certain inalienable rights, among which are life, liberty and the pursuit of happiness," crossed the Jordan from colonial bondage to national freedom.

Then, as in a photograph, will be held up to the world's gaze our own broad land; this Atlantic Slope and that Pacific Slope, with that boundless intervening valley "well watered everywhere like the land of Egypt, as thou comest unto Zoar;" blessed with "the precious things of heaven, the dew and the deep that coucheth beneath, the precious fruits brought forth by the sun, the precious things put forth by the moon, the chief things of the ancient mountains and the precious things of the earth and fullness thereof, and the good-will of Him that dwelt in the bush"; that imperial platform of commonwealths, inseparably interlocked together, ribanded to one another by majestic rivers and pressed down in their places by everlasting mountains, swarming with forty millions of people, humming with the music of countless industries, adorned with arts that vie with those of the nations across the sea, dotted over with schools, seminaries, colleges and universities where out sons are "as plants growing up in their youth and our daughters like corner-stones polished after the similitude of a palace," abounding from lake to gulf and from ocean to ocean with Sabbath-schools, and with church edifices whose spires point to heaven, and glorified with countless hospitals and homes for the friendless, and other institutions of Christian charity:

A glorious land,
With broad arms stretched from shore to shore,
The proud Pacific chafes her strand,
She hears the loud Atlantic roar;
And nurtured in her ample breast,
How many a goodly prospect lies,
In nature's wildest grandeur drest,
Enameled with her loveliest dyes!

When the project for the celebration had taken practicable shape, and it had become certain that a great "international exposition" was to be held which should present an epitome of our national productions, a grouping of all the agencies, instrumentalities, elements, products and results of our American civilization, challenging the attention of the world to the condition of mechanic art and fine art, agricultural interests, educational institutions, literature and science among us, the question very naturally arose, *What of religion?* Is religion to be ignored as a thing of naught on such an occasion? Religion, in a land where nearly every seventh person occupies a seat at some evangelical communion-table; religion, that had so large an agency in the revolution; religion, that has done more for our civilization and for the common weal that any other agency, if not more than all the others put together—shall it have no part in the grand celebration, no voice in the general jubilee?

To ask the question was to answer it. No enlightened Christian but felt that the Church in our land would be chargeable with shameful remissness if it allowed the mere secularities of life to monopolize the honors of the hour, and refused or neglected to give God the glory. Accordingly, all, or nearly all, of the religious denominations in the country have taken measures in one way or another to call attention to their services severally in the great work of helping on the weal of the nation.

This being so, how could Presbyterians fail to take their part on such an occasion? How could they justify themselves to themselves and to the system they so fondly cherish if they alone remained inert, and, instead of blending their denominational zeal with their patriotism, allowed their fervor as citizens to monopolize all their thoughts and energies?

On such an occasion who will condemn, what magnanimous spirit will not commend the act, if we as Presbyterians accept the opportunity to inquire into and set forth the services rendered by Presbyterianism in the cause of our country?

There is no call upon us to disparage any other body of co-workers in the cause of human emancipation. If our Lutheran brethren remind us that the illustrious leader whose name they bear was the first in the great Reformation to smite and break the chain that held the human mind in bondage, we, with all our hearts, will thank God with them for the services which that heroic man was called to render. But for the Reformation led by Luther, there had been no Revolution led by Washington. And our Episcopal brethren may well glory in the fact that Washington was an Episcopalian, as was also the pre-eminent George Mason, successor of Washington as representative in the Virginia Convention in 1776. Nor will our

Baptist brethren, always the champions of liberty, civil and religious, forbid our glorying in our cause, for we glory with them in the name of Roger Williams, who, far in advance of his times, delivered the golden oracle, "The civil magistrate should restrain crime, but never control opinion," and whose biography has been faithfully recorded by a Presbyterian pen. "And John Wesley," writes Mr. Bancroft, "on getting the tidings of the battles of Lexington and Concord, thought that silence on his part would be a sin against God, against his country and against his own soul; and waiting but one day, he wrote severally to Dartmouth and Lord North"; and among other things he said:

> In spite of all my long-rooted prejudices, I cannot avoid thinking these an oppressed people asking for nothing more than their legal rights, and that in the most modest and inoffensive manner that the nature of the thing will allow.
>
> Is it common sense to use force toward the Americans? They are strong; they are valiant; they are one and all enthusiasts—enthusiasts for liberty—calm, deliberate enthusiasts.
>
> They are terribly united; they think they are contending for their wives, children and liberty.

As to the Puritans of New England, their heroic devotion, sacrifices and services are too well known and too widely acknowledged to fear assault from any quarter. Truth to history, indeed, constrains the record that the Puritanism of New England embosomed a large element of Presbyterianism. "It is estimated," writes Dr. Charles Hodge in his *Constitutional History of the Presbyterian Church in the United States of America*, "that about twenty-two thousand two hundred emigrants arrived in New England before 1640. Cotton Mather tells us that previous to that same year four thousand Presbyterians had arrived." In another place, when speaking of the union effected between the Congregationalists and Presbyterians in London about the year 1690, he says: "The same union, and on the same terms, had subsisted between these two denominations in New England for 'many decades of years'—that is, almost from the first settlement of the country."

Accordingly, Increase Mather begged King William to consider that "in New England they differ from other plantations; they are called Congregational and Presbyterian; so that such a governor will not suit with the people of New England, as may be very proper for other English plantations.

"Of the two thousand Presbyterian ministers cast out of the Church of England by the Act of Uniformity, a considerable number, it is said, found a refuge in New England."

The Rev. J. B. Dales, D. D., of the United Presbyterian Church, in his discourse at the Tercentenary Celebration of Presbyterianism,* held in Philadelphia in 1872, said:

> The Puritans of England were long after their rise unquestionably largely Presbyterian. Robinson distinctly affirmed that his church at Leyden, the mother-church of the Plymouth colony, was of the same government as the Protestant Church of France. Fourteen years before the landing of the Pilgrim Fathers in New England, Brewster was chosen an elder by the congregation; and when, nearly two years after, he was chosen to be an assistant of Robinson, he declined to administer the sacraments expressly on the ground that the ruling elder's office which he held did not entitle him to do that which he believed belonged to the minister or teaching elder.

> With this office and with these views, Brewster came to this country with the Plymouth colony, and thus he helped to form the Plymouth Church. Thenceforward for a long period, acting on this principle, the early churches of Salem, Charlestown, Boston and elsewhere in New England had ruling elders, while in 1646 and 1680 respectively all the ministers and an elder from each church met in synod at Cambridge, and by distinct act recognized the Presbyterian form of church government. They went so far as to adopt the Confession of Faith of the Westminster Assembly of Divines.

It is therefore abundantly evident that in the splendid patriotism of New England in the Revolution, Presbyterianism had a far from insignificant share.

As, then, from our Centennial heights we take a view of the teeming affluence of results that have issued from our Revolutionary struggle—results of material prosperity, of civil and religious freedom, happy severance of Church and State, of evangelical piety and missionary zeal—and with ample and thankful acknowledgments of all that is due to others—it is a privilege of Presbyterians which no one will question, to remind themselves and others of the services rendered by Presbyterianism in that momentous struggle.

# 2

# PRESBYTERIANISM: A REPRESENTATIVE REPUBLICAN FORM OF GOVERNMENT

Presbyterianism, strictly speaking, is a system of church government, and is not necessarily allied to any one system of doctrine. History, however, shows it so steadily inclining toward and so generally associated with the system of doctrine commonly styled Calvinistic as to suggest the existence of strong affinities between them.

For a Mr. Barnes writes, "Calvinism and Presbyterianism spring essentially from the same idea—the idea of government, of regularity, of order; the idea that God rules; that government is desirable; that things are and should be fixed and stable; that there is and should be law; that the affairs of the universe at large, the affairs of society and the affairs of individual should be founded on settled principles, and should not be left to chance and haphazard."

> Calvinism, though it seems to be, and though it is often represented as, a mere system of doctrine or of abstract dogmas having no philosophical foundation and no practical bearing, is, in fact, a system of government—a method and form in which the divine power is put forth in the administration of the affairs of the universe. It is based on the idea that God rules; that he has a plan; that the plan is fixed and certain;

that it does not depend on the fluctuations of the human will, on the caprice of the human heart, or on the contingencies and uncertainties of undetermined events in human affairs. It supposes that God is supreme; that he has authority; that he has a right to exercise dominion; that for the good of the universe that the right should be exercised, and that infinite power is put forth only in accordance with a plan.

JOHN CALVIN

CALVINISM, THOUGH IT SEEMS TO BE, AND THOUGH IT IS OFTEN REPRESENTED AS, A MERE SYSTEM OF DOCTRINE OR OF ABSTRACT DOGMAS HAVING NO PHILOSOPHICAL FOUNDATION AND NO PRACTICAL BEARING, IS, IN FACT, A SYSTEM OF GOVERNMENT—A METHOD AND FORM IN WHICH THE DIVINE POWER IS PUT FORTH IN THE ADMINISTRATION OF THE AFFAIRS OF THE UNIVERSE.

Presbyterianism is the carrying out of ideas of order, authority and law as manifested in government and in doctrine. And as a rule, Calvinism and Presbyterianism are found combined.

That there is a natural and strong affinity between Presbyterian and republican forms of government is a truth that secular historians have recognized and fully acknowledge.

"Calvinism," writes Mr. Bancroft, "is gradual republicanism."

"In Geneva, a republic on the confines of France, Italy and Germany, Calvin, appealing to the people for support, continued the career of enfranchisement by planting the institutions which nursed the minds of Rousseau, Necker and De Stael."

"It was to Geneva," writes Mr. Villers (quoted by Smythe), "that all the proscribed exiles who were driven from England by the intolerance of Mary came *to get intoxicated with republicanism*, and from this focus they brought back with them those *principles of republicanism* which annoyed Elizabeth, perplexed and resisted James and brought Charles to the deserved death of a traitor."

"The remains of the school of Melville," writes Dr. Ayton, "led on by Mr. William Scott and Mr. John Carmichael, were *favorable to a republic.*"

"Did a proud aristocracy," writes Mr. Bancroft, "trace its lineage through a highborn ancestry, the Republican Reformer with a loftier pride invaded the invisible world, and from the book of life brought down the record of the noblest enfranchisement decreed from all eternity by the King of kings."

"Calvin," writes Bishop Horsley, "was unquestionably in theory a republican. So wedded was he to this notion that *he endeavored to fashion the government of all the Protestant churches* upon republican principles."

"The school of Knox," writes Hallam, "was full of men breathing their Master's spirit. Their system of local and general assemblies infused, together with the *forms of a republic,* its energy and impatience of external control, combined with the concentration and unity of purpose that belong to the most vigorous government.

"Not merely in their representative assemblies, but in their pulpits, they perpetually remonstrated in no guarded language against the misgovernment of the court and even the personal indiscretions of the king."

To such an extreme did they carry their views of freedom that Andrew Melville, when summoned before the court to answer some so-called seditious utterances in the pulpit, declined to acknowledge its jurisdiction on the ground that he was responsible first to his presbytery.

Of the Scottish preachers Lord Macaulay writes: "They inherited the *republican* opinions of Knox."

Isaac Taylor calls republicanism *the Presbyterian principle.*

The late, able and distinguished Roman Catholic, Archbishop Hughes of New York, wrote:

> Though it is my privilege to regard the authority exercised by the General Assembly as usurpation, still I must say, with every man acquainted with the mode in which it is organized, that for the purposes of popular and political government its structure is little inferior to that of Congress itself. It acts on the principle of a radiating centre, and is without an equal or a rival among the other denominations of the country.

Very welcome testimony is this, from a very unexpected quarter. The fundamental principles of Presbyterianism embrace the following points:

1. The body of the people are, under God, the source and fountain of all the powers exercised in the government of the Church.
2. Only by the voice of the people can any incumbent find his way into official position.
3. In connection with the pastor, who has been elected by the people, certain people, elected for this purpose by their brethren, shall exercise

the functions of rulers over the church and congregation.

4. The government of the Church is to be administered in accordance with a constitution embracing principles derived from the word of God and agreed upon by the people, through those whom they have chosen to represent them.
5. All ministers hold perfect equality of rank among themselves, and as rulers, all preachers and ruling elders have equal authority in the governing assemblies of the Church.
6. The voice of the majority is the voice of the whole. This principle applies equally to any congregation in the choice of officers, and to any one of the local governing assemblies, and also to the whole aggregate Church.

"The radical principles of Presbyterian church government are that a larger part of the Church, or a representation of it, should govern a smaller; that in like manner a representation of the whole should govern and determine in regard to every part, and to all the parts united—that is, a *majority shall govern.*"

That this system is in close accord with that of the primitive Church ecclesiastical history testifies.

"Each individual church," writes Mosheim, "assumed to itself the rights of a little distinct *republic* or *commonwealth.*

"At length the churches of a province became associated much after the manner of confederate republics, so that the Christian community may be said thenceforward to have resembled one large commonweal, made up, like those of Holland and Switzerland, of many minor republics."

Speaking of the Presbyterian system, Alexander Henderson writes:

> Here is superiority without tyranny; for no minister has a papal or monarchical jurisdiction over his own flock, far less over other pastors and over all the congregations. Here is parity without confusion and disorder; for the pastors are in order before elders. Every particular church is subordinate to a presbytery, the presbytery to the synod, and the synod to the national assembly. Here is subjection without slavery; for the people are subject to the pastors and assemblies; yet there is no assembly wherein every particular church hath not interest and power.

Those who are familiar with the forms of the Greek, Roman and former French republics are aware of one marked distinction between them and our own, in the matter or *organization*. The former were exceedingly loose-jointed, while ours is as one body, "fitly joined together and compacted by that which every joint supplieth," legislative, executive, judicial, all distinct, yet working together as component parts of well-adjusted machinery. In the commonwealth we find township, country and State government compacted into a happy system of order, superiority and subordination; in the judiciary, court above court, from lowest to supreme; and above all, the national Congress and government.

So in our Church we have, first, the individual session, composed of men elected by the people—each church a little republic. Above the session is the presbytery, supervising all the church sessions, and composed of ministers and a lay representation from the several churches, equal and often superior in number to the ministers—another and larger republic. Next above is the synod, which is only a larger presbytery—another republic. And above all is the general assembly, which is the general presbytery, our ecclesiastical congress, our whole Church in general assembly convened.

The records of every session are annually reviewed and commended or censured by the presbytery to which it belongs. In like manner, the records of each presbytery are reviewed by the synod, and the records of each synod by the general assembly. A member of any one of our churches tried and censured by the session may appeal to the presbytery, and thence, if he will, to the synod, and thence to the general assembly. Thus the youngest and humblest member of the Presbyterian Church enjoys the inalienable privilege of having his case finally adjudicated by the *whole Church.*

It is obvious, therefore, that our church government is in singular harmony with the spirit and form of government in both the State and nation

# 3

# Presbyterianism: Odious to Tyrants

"Protestantism," writes Carlyle, "was a revolt against spiritual sovereignties, popes and much else. *Presbyterians* carried out the revolt *against earthly sovereignties.*" Queen Elizabeth detested "presbytery" because it held principles inconsistent with allegiance to her crown.

"She knew that the church of Geneva, which the Puritans declared to be their model, was not only essentially republican, but could not be perfectly established except in a republic."

"The Presbyterian clergy," writes Mr. Hallam, "individually and collectively displayed the intrepid and haughty spirit of the English Puritans. Though Elizabeth had, from policy, abetted the Scottish clergy in their attacks upon the civil administration, this connection itself had probably given her such an insight into their temper as well as their influence that she must have shuddered at the thought of seeing a *republican assembly* substituted for her faithful satraps, her bishops, so ready to do her bidding."

*King James* detested "presbytery." In Scotland, indeed, he had professed himself an enthusiastic Presbyterian. In the general assembly, with uplifted hands, in a rapture of enthusiasm, he exclaimed:

> I bless God that I was born in such a time as in the light of the gospel, and in such a place as to be king in such a Kirk, the sincerest Kirk in all the world.
>
> I charge you, my good people—ministers, elders, nobles, gentleman and barons—to stand to your purity, and I, forsooth, as long as I brook my life and crown, will maintain the same against all deadly.

KING JAMES

I CHARGE YOU, MY GOOD PEOPLE—MINISTERS, ELDERS, NOBLES, GENTLEMAN AND BARONS—TO STAND TO YOUR PURITY, AND I, FORSOOTH, AS LONG AS I BROOK MY LIFE AND CROWN, WILL MAINTAIN THE SAME AGAINST ALL DEADLY.

But when, having become king of England as well as of Scotland, he had crossed the border, "he found," to quote the words of Hallam, "a very different race of churchmen, well trained in the supple school of courtly conformity, and emulous flatterers of both his power and his wisdom."

In this state of things the king soon began to waver. His despotic instincts taught him where his interest lay. And while in this transition state it is said that one of his sturdy old chaplains, who feared God too well to be overmuch afraid of kings, treated His Majesty one Sabbath morning to a sermon on a text after his own name, James, first, sixth (James was the first of England and the sixth of Scotland): "He that wavereth is like a wave of the sea driven with the wind and tossed."

But the sermon did not save the king. On the second day of the Hampton Court Conference, while the learned and excellent Dr. Reynolds was speaking, Bancroft, bishop of London, fell on his knees and begged the king to stop the schismatic's mouth. As Reynolds proceeded King James broke in, exclaiming in his profane way:

"You are aiming at a Scots' presbytery, which agreeth as well with monarchy as God and the devil. Then Jack and Tom and Will and Dick shall meet, and at their pleasure censure me and my council. Then Will shall stand up and say, It must be thus. Then Dick shall reply and say, Nay, marry, but we will have it thus; and therefore I say, The king shall decide."

Then turning to the sycophants that fawned on him, he added: "I will make them conform or I will harry them out of the land, or else worse—only hang them, that's all."

On the third day the king advocated the high commission, inquisitorial oaths, and Whitgift, archbishop of Canterbury, exclaimed:

"Your Majesty speaks by the especial assistance of God's Spirit."

And Bancroft, bishop of London, fell on his knees and said: "My heart melteth for joy because God hath given England such a king as since Christ's time hath not been."

Charles I, a thorough despot, hated presbytery. The thought is brought out by Bancroft where, incidentally, he speaks of "The political character of Calvinism, which with one consent and with instinctive judgment the *monarchs* of that day *feared as republicanism,* and which Charles I declared a religion unfit for a gentleman," etc.

"Show me," said Charles, "any precedent where presbyterial government and regal were together without perpetual rebellions. And it cannot be otherwise, for the ground of their doctrine is anti-monarchical."

CHARLES I

SHOW ME, ANY PRECEDENT WHERE PRESBYTERIAL GOVERNMENT AND REGAL WERE TOGETHER WITHOUT PERPETUAL REBELLIONS. AND IT CANNOT BE OTHERWISE, FOR THE GROUND OF THEIR DOCTRINE IS ANTI-MONARCHICAL.

The king had a congenial instructor in his chaplain, Peter Heylin, D.D., who wrote a work under this title: *Aerius Redivivus; Or, The History of the Presbyterians, containing the Beginning, Progresse and Successes of that Active Sect, their Oppositions to Monarchical Governments,* etc. The volume ends as follows:

"Thus we have seen the dangerous doctrines and positions, the secret plots and open practices, the sacrileges, spoils and rapines, the tumults, murders and seditions, the horrid treasons and rebellions, which have been raised by the Presbyterians in most parts of Christendom for one hundred years and upward," etc., etc.

Dean Swift, speaking of those who took refuge in Geneva from persecution in England, says:

"When they returned, they were grown so fond of the government and religion of the place that they used all possible endeavors to introduce *both* into our country. From hence they proceeded to *quarrel with the kingly government* because the city of Geneva, to which their fathers had flown for refuge, was a commonwealth or government of the people."

The poet Dryden, a double apostate—an apostate from Cromwellian republicanism to the despotism of Charles II, and then from Puritanism to Romanism—wrote, as well he might:

> Quickened with fire below, your monsters breed
> In fenny Holland and in fruitful Tweed;
> And, like the *first,* the last affects to be
> Drawn from the dregs of a democracy.
> But as the poisons of the deadliest kind
> Are to their own unhappy coasts confined,
> So *presbytery,* in its pestilential zeal,
> *Can flourish only in a commonweal.*

# 4

# Presbyterian Spirit in Harmony with That of the Revolution

A reasonably thorough discussion of this theme would take us across the ocean and back through past centuries, since our earlier forefathers and many of the noblest of our Revolutionary champions came to us from other lands, and the principles that formed the life of the American struggle emerged to view and embodied themselves in action on many a foreign shore.

"A young French refugee," writes Mr. Bancroft, "skilled alike in theology and civil law, entering the republic of Geneva, and conforming its ecclesiastical discipline to the *principles of republican simplicity,* established a party of which Englishmen became members and new England the asylum."

"Calvinism was revolutionary. By the side of the eternal mountains, the perennial snows and arrowy rivers of Switzerland, it established a government without a king. It was powerful in France. It entered Holland, inspiring an industrious nation with heroic enthusiasm. It penetrated Scotland, and nerved its rugged but hearty envoy to resist the flatterers of Queen Mary. It infused itself into England, and placed its plebeian sympathies in strong resistance to the courtly hierarchy. Inviting every man to read the Bible, and teaching as a divine revelation the natural equality of man, it claimed freedom of utterance."

"It inspired its converts to cross the Atlantic and sail away from the traditions of the Church, from hereditary power, from the sovereignty of earthly kings, and from all dominion but that of the Bible and such as arose from natural reason and equity." In 1571 the French General Assembly met at Rochelle, with Theodore Beza as moderator. There were present at that Assembly the queen of Navarre, Henry, the Bourbon prince of Conde´, Prince Louis, count of Nassau, Admiral Coligny and other lords and gentlemen. That General Assembly represented and ruled over twenty-one hundred and fifth churches. In some of these churches there were ten thousand members.

Then came the massacre of St. Bartholomew, followed by the revocation of the Edict of Nantes, and this by every species of persecution and torture of which the Romish brain has been ever so fertile—plunder of property, burning of religious books, tearing of children from their parents, dragging of ministers to torture, breaking them on the wheel, killing them and throwing their bleeding corpses to dogs; some were roasted by slow fires, some were gashed with knives and some torn with red-hot pincers.

"No wonder these persecuted ones fled beyond the seas and sought shelter in foreign lands—five hundred thousand of them—some in England, some at the Cape of Good Hope and many in America. Of these last some went to New England and some to New York, but South Carolina became their chief resort—fugitives from Languedoc, Rochelle and Bordeaux and St. Quentin and the beautiful valley of Tours."

"Their church was in Charleston; and thither on every Lord's day, gathering from Cooper, and taking advantage of the ebb and flow of the tide, they might be seen, parents with their children, whom no bigot could now wrest from them, making their way in light skiffs through the tranquil scene."

"Other Huguenots established themselves on the banks of the Santee, in a region which has since been celebrated for affluence and refined hospitality."

"The United States are full of monuments of the emigrations from France. The son of Judith Manigault entrusted the vast fortune he had acquired to the service of the country that had adopted his mother. The hall in Boston where the eloquence of New England rocked the infant spirit of independence was the gift of the son of a Huguenot. On our frontier State the name of the oldest college bears witness to the wise liberality of the descendant of the Huguenots."

"The children of the Calvinists of France have reason to respect the memory of their ancestors."

The Netherlands, from the earliest times, had shown the spirit of revolt against the sins and tyrannies of Rome, and hence became a land of refuge for the persecuted in other European countries. And in successive generations, Waldenses, Albigenses, Bohemian Brothers and others fought there the fight of faith and leavened the general mind with Calvinistic principles. There the Bible became the textbook of the people. Forbidden to worship in the chapels, they went forth on the Lord's Day in vast processions into the fields; women and children gathered in a circle around the pulpit, and around them the men with arms in their hands, where, on some occasions for four hours, they listened and prayed and sung. Sometimes their preacher came galloping to the field on a fleet-footed and spirited horse, fired a pistol and preached the word from the saddle.

In 1562 the Netherlanders drew up a Confession of Faith. It was sent to Calvin for his approval and then printed in Dutch and German. It confessedly expressed the views generally maintained by believers dispersed throughout the Low Countries who desired to live according to the purity of the holy gospel of our Lord Jesus Christ.

Dutch Presbyterian Calvinism contributed a noble band of heroes to the cause of American freedom.

The first settlement on Manhattan Island, in 1623, consisted of thirty families, chiefly of Protestant fugitives from the well-scourged Belgian provinces. In want of a regular minister, two "consolers of the sick" held religious services among them. In 1628 a clergyman came, an elder was chosen and the Lord's Supper administered to fifty souls. Under the protection of the city of Amsterdam, a body of Waldenses emigrated to New Netherlands. When the Huguenot churches at Rochelle were razed, emigrants came in such numbers that public documents were sometimes issued in *French* as well as in Dutch and English, and the memory of the old Rochelle perpetuated by a New Rochelle in the land of their refuge.

Of Scotland, the land of Knox and the Melvilles, there is no need to speak. In their struggles with tyranny, the Scottish leaders

MANHATAN ISLAND

were driven to probe to the bottom the grave questions of the rights of man and the prerogatives of princes; and in America their children, the heirs of their courage and principles, found a sphere

GALLOWAY

for the practical application of those principles and the exercise of that courage.

To the trumpet-call of the Revolution so universal and cordial was the response of Presbyterians, that ardent devotees of King George, Lord North and Parliament could scarce see any one else in arms for the colonial cause but Presbyterians.

"Mr. Galloway, a prominent advocate of the government," writes Dr. Charles Hodge, "ascribed the revolt and revolution mainly to the action of the Presbyterian clergy and laity as early as 1764, when the proposition for a general synod emanated from a committee appointed for the purpose in Philadelphia. This was a great exaggeration and mistake, but it indicates the close connection between the civil and religious part of the controversy."

Another monarchist wrote:

"You will have discovered that I am no friend of the Presbyterians, and that I fix all the blame of these extraordinary American proceedings upon them.

"Believe me sir, the Presbyterians have been the chief and principal instruments in all these flaming measures; and they always do and ever will act against government from that restless and turbulent anti-monarchial spirit which has always distinguished them everywhere when they had, or by any means could assume, power, however illegally."

Indeed, so prominent and conspicuous was the part taken by Presbyterians as individuals and as a Church in the Revolutionary struggle that at the close of the war, rumors were very rife that projects were on foot to make Presbyterianism the religion of the new republic.

As we read in Gillett's history, "The Presbyterian Church occupied indeed a highly respectable position. Its ministers had been chaplains in the army. Its leading man, Dr. Witherspoon, had been a leader in the General Congress. It was, in fact, the only denomination which, from position and influence, could be considered in the light of a candidate for the special favors of the State."

The suspicion that such state connection was aimed at by the Presbyterians was so strong in certain quarters that the synod in 1783 put on her records a formal and emphatic repudiation of any such purpose or desire.

Colonel Barre having in an enthusiastic speech in parliament styled the Americans *Sons of Liberty,* the colonists caught up the title, and all through the land formed associations of Sons of Liberty, and the Sons of Liberty of New York went by the name of the *Presbyterian Junto.*

Let us quote again from Bancroft:

"Just after the peace of Paris the 'Heart of Oak Protestants' came over in great numbers and settled on the Catawba, in South Carolina. In Pennsylvania they peopled many counties. In Virginia they went up the valley of the Shenandoah and extended themselves into the upland region of North Carolina. Their training in Ireland had kept the spirit of liberty as fresh in their hearts as if they *had just been listening to the preaching of Knox or musing over the political creed of the Westminster Assembly.*"

"We shall find that the first voice publicly raised in America to dissolve all connection with Great Britain came, not from the Puritans of New England, nor the Dutch of New York, nor the planters of Virginia, *but from the Scotch-Irish Presbyterians.*"

"In 1683, just after the grant of East New Jersey, a proclamation unparalleled since Alva drove the Netherlands to independence put twenty thousand lives at the mercy of informers. After the insurrection of Monmouth, gibbets were erected in every village and soldiers entrusted with the execution of the laws; scarce a Presbyterian family in Scotland but was involved in proscriptions and penalties."

"Is it strange that Scotch Presbyterians of virtue, education and courage, blending a love of popular liberty with religious enthusiasm, hurried to East New Jersey in such numbers as to give to the rising commonwealth a character which a century and a half has not effaced?"

"In a few years a law of the commonwealth giving force to the common principle of the New England and the Scottish colonists established a system of free schools."

"Hearts glowed more warmly on the banks of the Patapsco. Its convenient proximity to the border counties of Pennsylvania and Virginia had at length been observed by *Scotch-Irish Presbyterians* and other bold and industrious men, and within a few years they had created the town of Baltimore."

When, in May, 1774, the messages from the old committee of New York, Philadelphia and Boston reached the inhabitants of the city and county of Baltimore, they, after consultation with the men of Annapolis, advocated suspending commerce with Great Britain and the West Indies, chose deputies to a colonial convention, recommended a Continental Congress, and sent cheering words to their "friends" at Boston as sufferers in the common cause. The supreme "Disposer of events," they wrote, "will terminate this severe trial of your patience in a happy confirmation of American freedom."

"For this spirited conduct Baltimore was applauded as the model, and its example kindled new life in New York."—*Bancroft.*

Respecting the Stamp Act, Mr. Bancroft writes:

"Our mother should remember that we are not slaves, said the Presbyterians of Philadelphia."

When news arrived of the passage through parliament of Townshend's bill taxing tea, glass, etc., according to Bancroft:

"Courage, Americans!" cried one of the famed 'Triumvirate' of Presbyterian lawyers, "Liberty, religion and science are on the wing to these shores. The finger of God points out a mighty empire to your sons. The savages of the wilderness were never expelled to make room for idolaters and slaves. The land we possess is the gift of Heaven to our fathers, and divine Providence seems to have decreed it to our latest posterity."

"The day dawns when the foundations of this mighty empire are to be laid by the *establishment of a regular American Constitution.* All that has hitherto been done seems to be little beside the collection of materials for this glorious fabric. The transfer of the European part of the family is so fast and our growth so swift that BEFORE SEVEN YEARS ROLL OVER OUR HEADS the first stone must be laid."

Such were the sentiments of the "Presbyterian Triumvirate" as early as 1768.

On the 20th of January, 1775, "the lords of the region" where the Watauga and the Forks of Holston flow into the Tennessee, *most of them Presbyterians of Scotch-Irish descent,* met in council near Abington.

"The news from Congress reaches them slowly, but on receiving it the spirit of freedom swept through their minds as naturally as the ceaseless forest wind sighs through the firs down the sides of the Black Mountains. They adhered unanimously to the association of Congress, and named a committee, with *Charles Cummings, their minister,* as its head.

"We explored," said the committee, "our uncultivated wilderness, bordering on many nations of savages and surrounded by mountains almost inaccessible. But even to these removed regions the hand of power hath pursued us to strip us of that liberty and property with which God, nature and the rights of humanity have vested us. We are willing to contribute all in our power, if applied constitutionally, but we cannot think of submitting our liberty or property to a venal British parliament or a corrupt ministry.

"We are deliberately and resolutely determined never to surrender any of our inestimable privileges to any power upon earth but at the expense of our lives. These are our real though unpolished sentiments of liberty and loyalty, and in the[m] we are resolved to live and die." *

The Hon. Gulian C. Verplanck of New York, in a public address, traced the origin of our Declaration of Independence to the National Covenant of Scotland.

Mr. William B. Reed of Philadelphia, himself an Episcopalian, wrote: "A Presbyterian royalist was a thing unheard of. The debt of gratitude which independent America owes to the dissenting clergy and laity *never can be paid.*"

"The rigid Presbyterians," writes Mr. Bancroft, "proved in America the supporters of religious freedom. They were true to the spirit of the great English dissenter who hated all laws that were formed

> To stretch the conscience, and to bind
> the native freedom of the mind.

"In Virginia the Presbytery of Hanover took the lead for liberty, and demanded the abolition of the establishment of the Anglican Church and the civil equality of every denomination."

---

*Bancroft

# 5

# The Westmoreland County Resolutions

How thoroughly Presbyterian in origin and character was the population scattered through Western Pennsylvania is known to all familiar with the early history of the State. At the time of the Revolution, Westmoreland County embraced nearly all the territory claimed by Pennsylvania west of the mountains.

When the news of the opening of the war at Lexington and Concord reached the people of Westmoreland, they cane together at Hanna's Town on the 16th of May, 1776, and passed the following resolutions:

"*Resolved, unanimously,* That the parliament of Great Britain by several late acts have declared the inhabitants of Massachusetts Bay to be in rebellion, and the ministry, by endeavoring to enforce those acts, have attempted to reduce the said inhabitants to a more wretched state of slavery than ever before existed in any state or country. Not content with violating their constitutional and chartered privileges, they would strip them of the rights of humanity, exposing lives to the wanton and unpunishable spirit of a licentious soldiery, and depriving them of the very means of subsistence.

"*Resolved, unanimously,* That there is no reason to doubt but the same system of tyranny and oppression will (should it meet with success in the Massachusetts Bay) be extended to every other part of America. It is therefore become the indispensable duty of every American, of every man who has any public virtue or love for his country, or any bowels for posterity, by every means which God has put in his power, to resist and oppose the execution of it; that for us, we will be ready to oppose it with our lives and fortunes. And the better to enable us to accomplish it, we will immediately form ourselves into a military body to consist of companies to be made up out of the several townships under the following association, which is declared to be the Association of Westmoreland County.

KING GEORGE III

"Possessed with the most unshaken loyalty to His Majesty King George III, whom we acknowledge to be our lawful and rightful king, and who we wish may long be the beloved sovereign of a free and happy people throughout the whole British empire, we declare to the world that we do not mean to deviate from the loyalty which we hold it to be our bounden duty to observe; but animated by the love of liberty, it is no less our duty to maintain and defend our just rights (which with sorrow we have seen of late wantonly violated in many instances by a wicked ministry and a corrupt parliament) and transmit them entire to our posterity, for which purpose we do agree and associate ourselves together:

"*First.* To arm and form ourselves into a regiment or regiments, and choose officers to command us in such proportion as shall be thought necessary.

"*Second.* We will, with alacrity, endeavor to make ourselves masters of the manual exercise and such evolutions as many be necessary to enable us to act as a body with concert, and to that end we will meet at such times and places as shall be appointed, either for the companies or the regiments, by the officers commanding each when chosen.

"*Third.* That should our country be invaded by a foreign enemy, or should troops be sent from Great Britain to enforce the late arbitrary acts of its parliament, we will cheerfully submit to military discipline, and to the utmost of our power resist and oppose them, or either of them, and we will coincide with any plan that may be formed for the defence of America in general or Pennsylvania in particular.

"*Fourth.* That we do not wish or desire any innovation, but only that things may be restored to and go on in the same way as before the era of the Stamp Act, when Boston grew great and America was happy. As a proof of this disposition, we will quietly submit to the laws by which we have been accustomed to be governed before that period, and will, in our several or associate capacities, be ready when called on to assist the civil magistrate in carrying the same into execution.

"*Fifth.* That when the British parliament shall have repealed their late obnoxious statutes, and shall have receded from their claim to tax us and make laws for us in every instance, or when some general plan of union and reconstruction has been formed and accepted by America, this our association shall be dissolved; but till then it shall remain in full force, and to the observation of it we bind ourselves by everything dear and sacred amongst men. No licensed murder! No famine introduced by law!"

That the meeting was effective, and that the association speedily developed into companies and regiments, is gathered from a letter from Arthur St. Clair, who lived in the Ligonier Valley, twenty miles from Hanna's Town, and who, on the 25th of May, wrote at length to Governor Penn about the troublesome boundary question, and made mention of the patriotic movement in the following paragraph:"We have nothing but musters and committees all over the country, and everything seems to be running into the greatest confusion. If some conciliating plan is not adopted by the Congress, America has seen her golden days; they may return, but they will be preceded by sense of horror. An association is formed in this county for the defence of American liberty. I got a clause added by which

IF SOME CONCILIATING PLAN IS NOT ADOPTED BY THE CONGRESS, AMERICA HAS SEEN HER GOLDEN DAYS; THEY MAY RETURN, BUT THEY WILL BE PRECEDED BY SENSE OF HORROR.

WILLIAM PENN

they bind themselves to assist the civil magistrates in the execution of the laws they have been accustomed to be governed by."

The Hanna's Town resolutions on a first reading scarcely seem to deserve the honor of a centennial celebration. There is a curiously mixed flavor of loyalty and rebellion in them, and they certainly do not constitute a declaration of independence, as has been claimed. When read in connection with the history of the times when they were adopted, however, it will be found that they were singularly bold and defiant. No public gathering held in the colonies during the year 1775 went further in the direction of independence unless it was the Mecklenburg meeting. The farmers of Westmoreland really laid down an ultimatum to the British government, and pledged themselves to resist its authority by force of arms until their demands for the repeal of all oppressive measures were complied with.

# 6

# The Mecklenburg Declaration

Of the population of Mecklenburg County and the adjacent regions Washington Irving writes in his *Life of Washington*:

"In this part of the State was a hardy Presbyterian stock, the Scotch-Irish, as they were called, having emigrated from Scotland to Ireland and thence to America, and were said to possess the impulsiveness of the Irishman with the dogged resolution of the Covenanter. The early history of the colonies abounds with instances of this spirit among the people. 'They always behaved insolently to their governors,' complained Governor Barrington

In this part of the State was a hardy Presbyterian stock, the Scotch-Irish, as they were called, having emigrated from Scotland to Ireland and thence to America....

Washington Irving

in 1731; 'some they have driven out of the country, at other times *they set up a government of their own choice* supported by men under arms.'"

The following is Mr. Bancroft's account of the "Mecklenburg Declaration," as given in the seventh volume of his *History of the United States*, beginning at page 370:

"The people of the county of Mecklenburg had carefully observed the progress of the controversy with Britain, and during the winter political meetings had repeatedly been held in Charlotte. That town had been chosen for the seat of the Presbyterian college which the legislature of North Carolina had chartered, but which the king had disallowed; and it was the center of the culture of that part of the province. The number of houses in the village was not more than twenty, but the district was already well settled by herdsmen, who lived apart on their farms.

"Some time in May, 1775, they received the news of the address which in the preceding February had been presented to the king by both houses of parliament, and which declared the American colonies to be in a state of actual rebellion. This was to them the evidence that the crisis in American affairs was come, and the people proposed among themselves to abrogate all dependence on the royal authority. But the militia companies were sworn to allegiance; and 'how,' it was objected, 'can we be absolved from our oath?' 'The oath', it was answered, 'binds only while the king protects.' At the instance of Thomas Polk, the commander of the militia of the county, two delegates from each company were called together in Charlotte as a representative committee. Before their consultations had ended, the message of the innocent blood shed at Lexington came up from Charleston and inflamed their zeal. They were impatient that their remoteness forbade their direct activity; had it been possible, they would have sent a hundred bullocks from their fields to the poor of Boston. No minutes of the committee are known to exist, but the result of their deliberations, framed with peculiar skill, precision of language and calm comprehensiveness, remains as the monument of their wisdom and courage. Of the delegates to that memorable assembly the name of Ephraim Brevard should be remembered with honor by his countrymen. He was one of a numerous family of patriot brothers, and himself in the end fell a martyr to the public cause. Trained in the college at Princeton, ripened among the brave Presbyterians of Middle Carolina, he digested the system which was then adopted, and which formed in effect a declaration of independence as well as a complete system of government. 'All laws and commissions confirmed by or derived from the authority of the king or parliament,' such are the bold but well-considered words of these daring statesmen, 'are annulled and vacated; all commissions, civil and military, heretofore granted by the Crown to be exercised in the colonies, are void; the provincial Congress of each province, under the direction of the great Continental Congress, is invested with all legislative and executive powers within the respective provinces, and no other legislative or executive power does or can exist at this time in any part of these colonies. As all former laws are now suspended in this province and the Congress has not yet provided others, we judge it necessary for the better preservation of good order to form certain rules and regulations for the internal government of this county until laws shall be provided for us by the Congress.'

"In accordance with these principles, the freemen of the county formed themselves into nine military companies and elected their own officers. Judicial powers were conferred on men to be singled out by the vote of the companies, two from each of them, the while number of eighteen constituting a court of appeal. The tenure alike of military and civil officers was 'the pleasure of their several constituents.' All public and county taxes, all quit-rents to the

Crown were sequestered, and it was voted that persons receiving new commissions from the king or exercising old ones should be dealt with as enemies of the country.

"The resolves were made binding on all, and were to be enforced till the provincial Congress should provide otherwise, or, what they knew would never take place, till the British parliament should resign its arbitrary pretensions with respect to America. At the same time, the militia companies were directed to provide themselves with arms, and Thomas Polk and Joseph Kennedy were specially appointed to purchase powder, lead and flints.

"Before the month of May had come to an end the resolutions were signed by Ephraim Brevard as clerk of the committee, and were adopted by the people with the determined enthusiasm which springs from the combined influence of the love of liberty and of religion. Thus was Mecklenburg County, in North Carolina, separated from the British empire. The resolves were transmitted with all haste to be printed in Charleston, and as they spread through the South they startled the royal governors of Georgia and North Carolina. They were dispatched by a messenger to the Continental Congress that the world might know their authors had renounced their allegiance to the king of Great Britain, and had constituted a government for themselves.

"The messenger stopped on his way at Salisbury, and there, to a crowd round the court-house, the resolves were read and approved. The western counties were the most populous part of North Carolina, and the royal governor had flattered himself and the king with the fullest assurance of their support. 'I have no doubt,' said he, 'that I might command their best services at a word on an emergency. I consider I have the means in my own hands to maintain the sovereignty of this country to my royal master in all events.' And now he was obliged to transmit the deliberate, consistent and well-considered resolutions of Mecklenburg, which he described as the boldest of all, 'most traitorously declaring the entire dissolution of the laws and constitution and setting up a system of rule and regulation subversive of His Majesty's government.'"

The full text of the Mecklenburg Declaration is as follows:

"1. *Resolved,* That whosoever, directly or indirectly, abetted, or in any way, form or manner countenanced, the unchartered and dangerous invasion of our rights, as claimed by Great Britain, is an enemy to this country, to America, and to the inherent and inalienable rights of man.

"2. *Resolved,* That we, the citizens of Mecklenburg county, do hereby dissolve the political bonds which have connected us to the mother country, and hereby absolve ourselves from all allegiance to the British Crown, and abjure all political connection, contract or association with that nation, who have wantonly trampled on our rights and liberties and inhumanly shed the blood of American patriots at Lexington.

"3. *Resolved,* That we do hereby declare ourselves a free and independent people; are, and of right ought to be, a sovereign and self-governing association, under the control of no power other than that of our God and the general government of the Congress; to the maintenance of which we solemnly pledge to each other our mutual co-operation and our lives, our fortunes and our most sacred honor.

"4. *Resolved,* That as we now acknowledge the existence and control of no law or legal officer, civil or military, within this county, we do hereby ordain and adopt as a rule of life, all, each and every of our former laws, wherein, nevertheless, the Crown of Great Britain never can be considered as holding rights, privileges, immunities or authorities therein.

"5. *Resolved,* That it is further desired that all, each and every military officer in this county is hereby reinstated in his former command and authority, he acting conformably to these regulations.

And that every member present of this delegation shall henceforth be a civil officer, namely: A justice of the peace in the character of a 'committeeman', to issue process, hear and determine all matters of controversy according to the said adopted laws, and to preserve peace, union and harmony in said county, and to use every exertion to spread the love of country and fire of freedom throughout America, until a more general and organized government be established in this province."

On December 7, 1819, Captain James Jack certified that he was appointed to carry the declaration to Congress; that he stopped at Salisbury, where Colonel Kennon, an attorney, read the resolutions in open court; that he only heard of one person, a Mr. Beard, who opposed them; and that he went on to Philadelphia and delivered the declaration.

The royal governor of the province, on the 30th of June, 1775, wrote as follows to the colonial secretary of Great Britain:

> The resolves of the committee of Mecklenburg, which your lordship will find in the enclosed newspaper, surpass all the horrid and treasonable publications the inflammatory spirits of this continent have yet produced; and your lordship may depend its authors and abettors will not escape my notice whenever my hands are sufficiently strengthened to attempt the recovery of the lost authority of the government.
>
> A copy of these resolves, I am informed, *was sent off to the Congress at Philadelphia* as soon as they were passed in the committee.

Then, on the 8th of August, 1775, he issued a proclamation in which he said:

> Whereas I have seen a most infamous publication in the 'Cape Fear Mercury,' importing to be the resolves of a set of people styling themselves a Committee of the County of Mecklenburg, most traitorously declaring *the entire dissolution of laws, government and constitution* of this country, and setting up a system of rule and regulation repugnant to the laws and subversive of His Majesty's government.

The coincidence of language and phrase between the Mecklenburg and national declarations will surprise no one familiar with the political writings and speeches of those times, where such phrases constantly recur.

John Adams

The silence of Congress respecting this declaration, and the fact that both Jefferson and John Adams knew nothing of it, are easily explained. The messenger who conveyed to Philadelphia the report of the Mecklenburg proceedings delivered that report to the North Carolina delegates. It was the business of those delegates to present this to Congress. But as Congress at this time shrank from the thought of independence, and three months after this unanimously and in the humblest terms petitioned King George for redress of grievances, what more likely than that the Carolina delegates looked upon the Mecklenburg movement as a hasty act of a few enthusiasts, and refrained from so much as mentioning the matter in Congress:

As late as August, 1775, Mr. Jefferson said: "I would rather be in dependence on Great Britain, properly limited, than on any nation on earth, or than *on no nation.*"

Washington said in May 1776, "When I took command of this army (June 1775), *I abhorred the idea of independence.*"

As to John Adams, so far as we can learn from Bancroft, his first public word in favor of independence was long subsequent to May 1775.

Whatever, then, is uncertain, this is unquestionable, that the Presbyterians of Mecklenburg in May 1775, far in advance of Congress and in advance of the rest of the country, passed resolutions

I WOULD RATHER BE IN DEPENDENCE ON GREAT BRITAIN, PROPERLY LIMITED, THAN ON ANY NATION ON EARTH, OR THAN ON NO NATION.

THOMAS JEFFERSON

which the royal governor Martin, in June of that year, could very justly stigmatize as "treasonable," and in August following could proclaim as "declaring the dissolution of the laws, government and constitution of the country, and the setting up of a system of rule and regulation repugnant to the laws and subversive of His Majesty's government."

Mr. Bancroft is more than justified in his declaration that "the first voice publicly raised in America to dissolve all connection with Great Britain came, not from the Puritans of New England, nor the Dutch of New York, nor the planters of Virginia, *but from the Scotch-Irish Presbyterians.*"

# 7

# Presbyterian Zeal and Suffering

The zeal of Presbyterians during the war exposed them to special cruelties at the hands of the British soldiery. Among the foremost patriots of that day was the Rev. James Caldwell, pastor of the Presbyterian church of Elizabethtown, N.J.

"Descended from the Huguenots," writes the Rev. Dr. Sprague in his *Annals*, feeling of opposition to tyrants. Connected with his congregation were the Daytons, the Ogdens, Francis Barber, William Crane, Oliver Spencer, Elias Boudinot, William Livingston, Abram Clark, and others who became eminent for their wisdom, piety, valor and patriotism."

When the news of the passage of the Declaration of Independence reached the New Jersey brigade, of which he was chaplain, the men were called together, and Parson Caldwell gave this toast: "Harmony, honor and all prosperity to the free and independent United States of America; wise legislators, brave and victorious armies, both by sea and land, to the United States of America." His church was given up to be used as a hospital for the sick. Its bell sounded the alarm on the approach of the foe.

In an attack upon Springfield, when the wadding of the patriots gave out, Caldwell ran to the Presbyterian church; and returning with his arms and pockets filled with "Watts' Psalms and Hymns," he scattered them among the soldiers, exclaiming, "Now, boys, give them Watts!"

In vexation at his patriotism, British officers offered large rewards for his capture. Failing in this, the British soldiery set fire to his church and shot his wife through the window of her own room in the midst of her nine children, dragged her bleeding corpse into the street and laid the house and other surrounding buildings in ashes. The following poem by Bret Harte tells the story:

Here's the spot. Look around you.
    Above on the height
Lay the Hessians encamped.
    By that church on the right
Stood the gaunt Jersey farmers.
    And here ran a wall.
You may dig anywhere, and you'll
    turn up a ball.
Nothing more. Grasses spring,
    waters run, flowers blow
Pretty much as they did ninety-three
    years ago.
Nothing more did I say? Stay one
    moment; you've heard
Of Caldwell, the parson, who once preached the word
Down at Springfield? What, no? Come, that's bad!
    Why, he had
All the Jerseys aflame. And they gave him the name
Of the "rebel high priest." He stuck in their gorge,
For he loved the Lord God, and he hated King George.
He had cause, you may say. When the Hessians that day
Marched up with Knyphausen, they stopped on the way
At the 'Farms', where his wife, with a child in her arms,
Sat alone in the house. How it happened none knew
But God and that one of the hireling crew
Who fired the shot. Enough! There she lay,

And Caldwell the chaplain, her husband, away.
Did he preach? Did he pray? Think of him as you stand
By the old church to-day; think of him and that band
Of militant ploughboys. See the smoke and the heat
Of that reckless advance, of that straggling retreat!
Keep the ghost of that wife, foully slain, in your view,
And what could you, what should you, what would *you* do?
Why, just what *he* did. They were left in the lurch
For the want of more waddling. He ran to the church,
Broke the door, stripped the pews,
    and dashed out into the road
With his arms full of hymn-books,
    and threw down his load at their feet.
Then above all the shouting and shots
Rang his voice: "Put Watts into 'em! Boys, give 'em Watts!"
And they did. That is all. Grasses spring, flowers blow
Pretty much as they did ninety-three years ago.
You may dig anywhere, and you'll turn up a ball,
But not always a hero like this; and that's all.

Dr. Thomas Smyth writes: "The battles of the Cowpens, of King's Mountain, and also the severe skirmish known as Huck's Defeat, are celebrated as giving a turning point to the contests of the Revolution. General Morgan, who commanded at the Cowpens, was a Presbyterian elder. General Pickens, who made all the arrangements for the battle, was a Presbyterian elder, and nearly all under their command were Presbyterians. In the battle of King's Mountain Colonel Campbell, Colonel James Williams, Colonel Cleveland, Colonel Shelby and Colonel James Williams, Colonel Sevier were all Presbyterian elders, and the body of their troops were from Presbyterian settlements. At Huck's Defeat, in York, Colonel Bratton and Major Dickson were both elders in the Presbyterian Church. Major Samuel Morrow, who was with Colonel Sumpter in four engagements and took part in many other engagements, was for about fifty years a ruling elder in the Presbyterian Church.

"It may also be mentioned that Marion, Huger and other distinguished men of Revolutionary memory were of Huguenot—that is, of full-blooded Presbyterian—descent."

On this point we find the following in the lamented Gillett's *History of the Presbyterian Church in the United States*:

"In initiating the Revolution and in sustaining the patriotic resistance of their countrymen to illegal tyranny, the ministers of the Presbyterian Church bore a conspicuous, and even foremost, part. Throughout that most trying and disastrous period through which the Church and country had as yet been called to pass they proved themselves alike faithful to both.

"They preached the duty of resisting tyrants. They cheered their people in the dreary period of conflict by inspiring lofty trust in the God of nations.

"Among those who advocated the cause of the colonists and strengthened the patriotic zeal by Christian principle were Dr. Witherspoon, Patrick Alison in Baltimore, William Tennent in Charlestown, George Duffield in Philadelphia, John Miller at Dover, James Waddell and John Blair Smith in Virginia.

"John Carmichael preached at their request to the militia of Lancaster. The discourse of Miller of Dover, who was bold in the expression of his patriotic ardor, was especially remarkable. Several days before the Declaration of Independence he so far anticipated the spirit of that decisive measure as to address his people from that significant test, 'We have no part in David, nor any inheritance in the son of Jesse: to your tents, O Israel!'

"Robert Davidson, pastor of the First Presbyterian Church of Philadelphia at the commencement of the war, preached before several military companies from the text, 'For there fell down many slain because the war was of God.' A fortnight after, it was repeated before the troops at Burlington. 'Of John Craighead it is said, He fought and preached alternately.' At the commencement of the war he raised a company from the members of his charge and joined Washington's army in New Jersey. His friend, Dr. Cooper of the Middle Spring church, is also said to have been captain of a company. He preached 'before Colonel Montgomery's battalion under arms' near Shippensburg, Pennsylvania, August 31, 1775, a sermon entitled 'Courage in a Good Cause.'

"Dr. King of Conococheague was eminent for his patriotic zeal. He not only volunteered and went as chaplain to the battalion which marched from his region, but many were the addresses which he delivered to in spirit the hearts of the people in their devotion to the cause of the country.

"In one of his sermons he said: 'Subjection is demanded of us, but it is not the constitutional subjection which we are bound to pay. It is not a legal subjection to the king they would bring us to—that we already acknowledge—but it is a subjection to the British parliament or to the people of Great Britain. They are not our lords or masters; they are no more than our brethren and fellow-subjects. They call themselves, and it has been usual to call them, the *mother-country*. But this is only a name; and if there was anything in it, one would think that it should lead them to treat us like children. But is it fatherly or motherly to strip us of everything, to rob us of every right and privilege, and then to whip and dragoon us with fleets and armies till we are pleased? No. As the name does not belong to them, so their conduct shows that they have no right to claim it. We are on an equal footing with them in all respects—with respect to government and privileges—and therefore their usurpation ought to be opposed. Nay, when the king uses the executive branch of government, which is in his hand, to enable one part of his subjects to lord it over and oppress another, it is a sufficient ground for our applying to the laws of nature for our defence. "'But this is the case with us. We have no other refuge from slavery but those powers which God has given us and allowed us to use in defence of our dearest rights; and I hope he will bless our endeavors and give success to this oppressed people, and that the wicked instruments of all these distractions shall meet their due reward. I earnestly wish that in such troublous times, while we plead for liberty, a proper guard may be kept against any turbulent or mobbish outbreak, and that unanimity may be universal both in council and in action, and that we may still have an eye to the great God who has some important reasons for such severe corrections. Let us look to the rod and him that hath appointed it. Let us humble ourselves before him daily for our sins and depend upon him for success. If he be against us, in vain do we struggle. If the Lord be for us, though a host should encamp against us, we need not be afraid.'"

In one of the darkest hours of the strife, after the repulse in Canada, he said in a funeral discourse on the death of Montgomery:

"Surely we have still reason for the exercise of faith and confidence in God that he will not give up a people to the unlimited will and power of others who have done all they could to avert the calamity, and who so strenuously adhered to the course of reason and humanity—a people who have been attacked with unprovoked violence and driven with the greatest reluctance to take up arms for their defence—a people whom he himself, by a series of gracious actings, hath gradually led on to this condition. Therefore, when these are our circumstances, we may rationally judge that God is not an unconcerned spectator, but that he sees and will reward the persecutors.

"Many things, indeed, seem to be against us—a very great and powerful enemy, who have long been trained to victory; their numerous and savage allies, who, having lost their liberty, would have others in the same condition; our weakness and inexperience in war; internal enemies; the loss of many of our friends and a beloved and able general. But let not these destroy our hopes or dampen our spirits. To put too much confidence in man is the way to provoke God to deprive us of them. This may perhaps be the darkness which precedes the glorious day.... It is agreeable to God's method to bring low before he exalteth, to humble before he raises up. Let us trust in him and do our duty, and commit the event to His determination who can make these things to be for us which, by a judgment of sense, we are ready to say are against us."

In a similar strain did he exhort the soldiers marching to the field or address the people who remained behind. "Be thou faithful unto death" was the text of one of his discourses. "There is no soldier," he said, "so truly courageous as a pious man. There is no army so formidable as those who are superior to the fear of death. Consequently, no one qualification is more necessary in a soldier than true religion." These words were accompanied by the tender counsels of a pastor whose affections followed his men to the scenes of danger and death. With the greatest earnestness he urged them to watch over their own souls, and not to bring dishonor on the cause to which they were attached.

While several of the Presbyterian ministers performed service and led companies to the field, a large number were engaged as chaplains in the army. Alexander McWhorter, afterward Dr. McWhorter, of Newark, was chaplain of Knox's brigade while it lay at White Plains, and often had General Washington among his hearers. James F. Armstrong, afterward of Elizabethtown, joined a volunteer company before his licensure, and soon after he was ordained was appointed by Congress "chaplain of the second brigade of the Maryland forces." Adam Boyd was chaplain of the North Carolina brigade. Daniel McCalla was sent to Canada as chaplain with General Thompson's forces at the commencement of hostilities. Dr. John Rodgers was chaplain of Heath's brigade.

George Duffield, in connection with Mr. (afterward Bishop) White, was employed as chaplain of the Colonial Congress.

"It was not infrequently that the minister of peace felt called upon to engage in active service in the armies of his country, and not a few of the young men who had won distinction in the use of carnal weapons became afterward still more eminent in the service of the gospel. When an unusual number of his people had been drafted to serve in the militia, James Latta, of Chestnut Level, with a view to encourage them, took his blanket, shouldered his knapsack and accompanied them on their campaign.

"Samuel Eakin, of Penn's Neck, was a strong Whig and the idol of the soldiers. Gifted with extraordinary eloquence and accounted scarcely inferior to Whitefield, he was ever on the alert to kindle the patriotic zeal of his countrymen. When there were military trainings, or the soldiers were ordered to march, he was present to address them and thrill them by his eloquence.

"John Blair Smith, teacher, and afterward president of Hampden-Sidney College, was chosen captain of a company of students, and after the battle of Cowpens hurried to join the retreating army, and was only dissuaded by the remonstrances of the commanding officer, who represented to him that his patriotic speeches at home would be far more valuable than his services in the camp.

"James Hall, of North Carolina, subsequently the pioneer missionary in the valley of the Mississippi, was selected as leader, and accepted the command, of a company formed mainly from his own congregation, whom his fervid and pathetic appeals had inspired to arm against Cornwallis. Such was his reputation that he was offered the commission of brigadier-general.

"When Tarleton and his British dragoons spread consternation throughout the surrounding valley of Virginia, William Graham, John Brown and Archibald Scott exhorted stripling youths of their congregations—their elder brethren were already with Washington—

to rise, join their neighbors and dispute the passage of the invader and his legion at Rockfish Gap, on the Blue Ridge. Graham was the master-spirit, but he was heartily supported by his co-presbyters. On one occasion, when there was backwardness to enlist, he had his own name enrolled. The effect was such that the company was immediately filled, and he was unanimously chosen captain.

"It is worthy of mention that Dr. Ashbel Green, many years before he aspired to be an ecclesiastical leader, had obtained the distinction of orderly sergeant in the militia of the Revolutionary period, and had risked his life in the cause of his country. Dr. Moses Hoge served for a time, previous to entering the ministry, in the army of the Revolution. Dr. John Brown, president of Georgia University, had at the early age of sixteen exchanged the groves of the academy for the noise and bustle of the camp, and fought with intrepid spirit by the side of Sumter his country's battles. Dr. Asa Hillyer, of Orange, N.J. while a youth, assisted his father, a surgeon in the Revolutionary army. Joseph Badger was in the battle of Bunker Hill, and served as soldier, baker, nurse, etc., in Arnold's expedition to Canada.

"James White Stephenson, of South Carolina, teacher of Andrew Jackson, served throughout the war, and on one occasion had his gun shivered in his hand by the enemy's shot, which glanced and killed the man who stood by his side. Lewis Feuilleteau Wilson, who studied medicine before his attention was directed to theology, served for several years as a surgeon in the Continental army. Simpson, of Fishing Creek, S.C., encouraged his people to deeds of heroism or patient endurance, and was himself found bearing arms, and was in several engagements. Joseph Alexander, of the same State, was often a fugitive from his own home, while he offered his dwelling at all times as a hospital for sick or wounded soldiers. Jonas Coe, one of the early members of the Albany presbytery, joined the army, along with his father and four brothers, while yet a youth of sixteen. Robert Marshall, afterward an eloquent minister in Kentucky, was in six general engagements, one of which was the hard-fought battle of Monmouth. James Turner, the eloquent Virginian preacher, could boast that at the early age of seventeen he had seen service in the Revolutionary army.

"These are but a few of that large band identified with the interests of the Presbyterian Church, and then, or at a later period, serving at her altar, who freely risked their lives in the service of their country. Whether in the bosom of their own congregations or serving the camp, they were animated by the same devotion to the cause of God and their native land. Their message everywhere was welcome. The soldier was inspired to bolder courage by the look and words of his own pastor or the pulpit exhortations of those who shared his hardships and his perils. The camp betrayed the presence of a conservative influence, which checked the vices which are wont to be indigenous to it, while many who never listened to the gospel before were privileged to hear it at a crisis when at every hour they stood in peril of their lives.

"To the privations, hardships and cruelties of the war the Presbyterians were pre-eminently exposed. In them the very essence of rebellion was supposed to be concentrated, and by the wanton plunderings and excesses of the marauding parties they suffered severely. Their Presbyterianism was *prima facie* evidence of guilt. A house that had a large Bible and David's Psalms in metre in it was supposed, as a matter of course, to be tenanted by rebels. To sing 'Old Rouse' was almost as criminal as to have leveled a loaded musket at a British grenadier.

"To the Presbyterian clergy the enemy felt an especial antipathy. They were accounted the ringleaders of rebellion. For them there was often not so much safety in their own dwellings as in the camp. When their people were scattered, or it was no longer safe to remain among them, the only alternative was to flee or join the army; and this alternative was often presented. Not infrequently the duty of the chaplain or the pastor exposed him to dangers as great as those which the common soldier was called to meet. There was risk of person, sometimes capture, and sometimes loss of life. Some ministers fled for safety. Dr. Rodgers was forced to absent himself from New York till the close of the war; McKnight, of Shrewsbury, N.J. was carried off a captive; Richards, of Rahway, N.J. took warning and fled; Dr. Buell, of East Hampton, L.I., who remained at his post,

BATTLE OF BREED'S HILL 1775

repeatedly ran imminent risks even from the men whom his wit and urbanity finally disarmed.

"Duffield was saved from capture at Trenton only by the timely warning of a friendly Quaker. At one time, while the enemy were on Staten Island, he preached to the soldiers in an orchard on the opposite side of the bay. The forks of a tree served him for a pulpit; but the noise of the singing attracted the notice of the enemy, and soon the voice of praise was interrupted by the whistling of balls. But the preacher, undismayed by the danger, bade his hearers retire behind a hillock, and there finished his sermon. Daniel McCalla was confined for several months in a loathsome prison-ship near Quebec. Nehemiah Greenman, of Pittsgrove, N.J., fled to the wilderness to escape the indignities so largely dealt out by the enemy to the Presbyterian ministers. Azel Roe, of Woodbridge, N.J., taken prisoner by the enemy, was confined for some time in the old sugarhouse. He came near having a fall in a small stream which the company had to ford on the way. The commanding officer kindly offered to carry Mr. Roe on his back. The offer was accepted; and the suggestion of Mr. Roe to the officer that he was priest-ridden now if never before so convulsed him with laughter that he was like to have dropped his load. Less merciful was the experience of John Rosburgh, of Allentown, N.J., first a private soldier and afterward chaplain of a military company formed in his neighborhood, and who was shot down in cold blood by a body of Hessians to whom he had surrendered himself a prisoner. There was a strange commingling of carnal and spiritual weapons in the experience of the camp. Joseph Patterson, one of the fathers of the presbytery of Redstone, had just knelt to pray under a shed when a board on a line with his head was shivered by the discharge of a rifle. Stephen B. Balch preached a sermon on subjection to the higher powers while General Williams, to the annoyance of royalists who were present, protected him with loaded pistols in his belt. The ministers on the frontiers, exposed to the attacks of the Indians, were compelled to go constantly armed. Thaddeus Dod, with his people, exchanged his church for the fort that had been built on the Monongahela. Samuel Doak, of the Holston settlements, paused in his sermon at the alarm of an attack, seized his rifle that stood by his side, and led his male hearers in pursuit of the foe.

"Not a few of the ministers of the Presbyterian Church were called into the civil service of their country. Jacob Green, the father of Dr. Ashbel Green, was a zealous patriot, and was elected, though contrary to his expressed wishes, a member of the provincial

Congress of New Jersey. He was chairman of the committee that drafted the constitution of the State.

"Henry Patillo was a member of the provincial Congress of North Carolina. J. J. Zubly was a delegate from Georgia to the Continental Congress.

"William Tennent of the Circular Church, Charleston, was a member of the provincial Congress of South Carolina, and amid the fearful emergencies of the period, and at different hours of the same day, he was occasionally, heard, in his church and in the State-house, addressing different audiences with equal animation on their temporal and spiritual interests. And not content with this, in company with William H. Drayton, he made the circuit of the middle and up-country of the State to stimulate the people to resistance.

"David Caldwell was a member of the convention that formed the State constitution of North Carolina. Kettletas, of Jamaica, was chosen a delegate to the New York convention; and Duffield, Rodgers, McWhorter and others were often consulted by civil and military officers in the trying crises of the Revolutionary period, and they were always prompt to render their services. Like Thomas Read, of Delaware, roused from his bed at midnight to describe the region which the army was to traverse, and in which he might act as a guide, they were never wanting when their country required their counsel or their aid.

"It is not strange that their course was regarded as specially obnoxious by the British troops. Their houses were plundered, their churches often burned and their books and manuscripts committed to the flames. The church of Midway, in Georgia, then Congregational, rendered itself obnoxious to the foe by its patriotic zeal. In November, 1778, a special detachment from Florida attacked the settlement, burned the church edifice, almost every dwelling-house, the crops of rice then in stacks, drove off the Negroes and horses, carried away the plate belonging to the planters, and outraged even the graves of the dead. Some of the members of the congregation were seized and imprisoned. Dr. McWhorter had removed to Carolina while the enemy, under Cornwallis, threatened the Southern country. Under the apprehension of danger, he fled with his family, and on his return found that his library, furniture and nearly all that he possessed had been sacrificed. Not less unfortunate were Elihu Spencer at Trenton, and David Caldwell and Hugh McAden of North Carolina. On many occasions the soldiers studiously destroyed all that they could not carry away, and the Presbyterian clergy were generally the special objects of vengeance.

"As might be expected, religion suffered greatly throughout the entire period of the war. The church edifices were often taken possession of by an insolent soldiery and turned into hospitals or prisons, or perverted to still baser uses as stables or riding schools. The church at Newtown had its steeple sawed off, and was used as a prison or guard-house till it was torn down and its siding used for the soldiers' huts. The church at Crumpond was burned to save its being occupied by the enemy. That of Mount Holly was burned by accident or design. The one at Princeton was taken possession of by the Hessian soldiers, and stripped of its pews and gallery for fuel. A fireplace was built, and a chimney carried up through its roof. Supposing it would be defended against him, Washington planted his cannon a short distance off and commenced firing into it. It was subsequently occupied by the American soldiers; and the close of the war found it dilapidated and open to the weather, while its interior was quite defaced and destroyed.

"The church of Westfield was injured by the enemy, and its bell carried off to New York. The church of Babylon, Long Island, was torn down by the enemy for military purposes. That of New Windsor was used as a hospital. This was the case also with the one at Morristown; and repeatedly in the morning, the dead were found lying in the pews. The one at Elizabethtown was made a hospital for the sick and disabled soldiers of the American army. Its bell sounded the note of alarm at the approach of the foe, while its floor was often the bed of the weary soldier, and the seats of its pews served as the table from which he ate his scanty meal. At length it was fired by the torch of the refugee in vengeance for the uses to which it had been devoted. The churches at New York were taken possession of by the enemy. Prisoners were confined in them, or they were used by the British officers for stabling their horses. Ethan Allen describes the filth that had accumulated in the one with which he was acquainted as altogether intolerable. More than fifty places of worship throughout the land were utterly destroyed by the enemy during the period of the war. The larger number of these was burned, others were leveled to the ground, while others still were so defaced or injured as to be utterly unfit for use. This was the case in several of the principal cities—at Philadelphia and Charleston as well as New York.

"But all did not escape. Caldwell of Elizabethtown was shot by a sentinel who is said to have been bribed by the British or the Tories, to whom he was especially obnoxious. Moses Allen, a classmate of President Madison at Princeton, pastor of the Midway church, Georgia, and chaplain of a regiment, was drowned near Savannah, February 8, 1779, in attempting to swim ashore from a prison-ship, the barbarous captain of which refused his friends boards for his coffin. And not a few others incurred hardships which, in all probability, shortened their days. It is certainly remarkable, considering their exposure and the almost venomous hatred with which they were regarded by the enemy, that among the Presbyterian ministers, the direct victims of the war were so few."*

**History of the Presbyterian Church in the United States of America.* E. H. Gillett, D. D. Vol. I, chap. 10.

# 8

# Formal Action of the Presbyterian Church

If, now, from such records as these we turn to what may be termed the official action of the Presbyterian Church in the Revolution, we shall find it full of ardent, high-toned patriotism.

Dr. Charles Hodge, in his Constitutional *History of the Presbyterian Church in the United States*, writes:

"One of the first exercises of the power claimed by parliament to impose taxes on America was the passage of the Stamp Act in 1764. The opposition to this measure was so general and vehement that the British government thought proper to repeal the act, though they accompanied the repeal with the strongest declarations of their right to tax the colonies at discretion. In the controversy relating to this subject the Synod of New York and Philadelphia publicly expressed their sympathy with their fellow-citizens. As soon as the repeal was known in this country, 'an overture was made by Dr. Alison that address be presented to our sovereign on the joyful occasion of the repeal of the Stamp Act, and thereby a confirmation of our liberties, and at the same time proposing a copy of an address for examination, which was read and approved,' but not recorded. The Synod also addressed a pastoral letter to the churches, filled with patriotic and pious sentiments. They remind the people that after God had delivered the country from the horrors of the French and Indian War, instead of rendering to him according to the multitude of his mercies, they had become more wicked than ever. 'The Almighty, thus provoked, permitted counsels of the most pernicious tendency both to Great Britain and her colonies. The imposition of unusual taxes, a severe restriction of our trade and almost total stagnation of business threatened us with universal ruin. A long suspense whether we should be deprived of or restored to a peaceable enjoyment of the inestimable privileges of English liberty filled every breast with painful anxiety.' They express their joy that government had been induced to resort to moderate measures instead of appealing to force, and call upon the people to bless God, who, notwithstanding their sins, had saved them from the horrors of a civil war. They finally earnestly exhort their people not to add to the common stock of guilt, but 'to be strict in observing the laws and ordinances of Jesus Christ, to pay a sacred regard to his Sabbaths, to reverence his holy name, and to adorn the doctrine of God our Savior by good works. We pray you,' say the Synod, 'to seek earnestly the saving knowledge of Christ and the internal power and spirit of religion. Thus many you hope for the continued kindness of a gracious Providence, and this is the right way to express gratitude to the Father of mercies for your late glorious deliverance. But persisting to grieve his Holy Spirit by a neglect of vital religion and a continuance of sin, you have reason to dread that a holy God will punish you yet seven times more for your iniquities.'"

As the indications of the coming conflict began to multiply, the Synod endeavored to prepare their people for the trial. Almost every year they appointed days for special prayer and fasting, and presented "the threatening aspect of public affairs as one of the most prominent reasons for their observance."

On the 17th of May, 1775, the Synod met in Philadelphia, and almost side by side with the Second Continental Congress. In that Congress sat George Washington, Benjamin Franklin, Samuel Adams, John Adams, Richard Henry Lee, Patrick Henry, John Jay and others, their worthy compeers. Nearby, in the Synod of New York and Philadelphia, then our General Assembly, sat Dr. Witherspoon, William Tennent, Dr. Rodgers, George Duffield, John Brainerd, Robert Cooper, for a time chaplain in the army; McWhorter, "who shared the councils of Washington on the memorable 26th of December, 1776, when the American troops crossed the Delaware, and who was afterward chaplain of Knox's brigade; James Caldwell, inheriting with his Huguenot blood a feeling of opposition to tyranny and tyrants; and Jedediah Chapman, the father of Presbyterianism in Central New York, and others besides, well worthy to stand in the foremost rank of American and Christian patriots."

"Foremost among them," writes Dr. Gillett, whom we have quoted above, "was the venerable Dr. Witherspoon, Scotch in accent and in strength of conviction, but American in feeling to his heart's core, and destined for six years to represent his adopted State in the general Congress, and draw up many of the most important state papers of the day.

WITH A CLEAR INTELLECT, A CALM JUDGMENT, INDOMITABLE STRENGTH OF PURPOSE AND A RESOLUTE AND UNFLINCHING COURAGE, HE COMBINED THAT CONSCIENTIOUS INTEGRITY AND RELIGIOUS FEELING WHICH MADE HIM AMONG HIS ASSOCIATES IN THE CHURCH WHAT WASHINGTON WAS IN THE FIELD, AND SECURED FOR HIM THE RESPECT AND VENERATION OF ALL.

DR. JOHN WITHERSPOON

"With a clear intellect, a calm judgment, indomitable strength of purpose and a resolute and unflinching courage, he combined that conscientious integrity and religious feeling which made him among his associates in the Church what Washington was in the field, and secured for him the respect and veneration of all."

The following record occurs in the minutes of this body: "The Synod, considering the present alarming state of public affairs, do unanimously judge it their duty to call all the congregations under their care to solemn fasting, humiliation and prayer, and for this purpose appoint the last Thursday of June next to be carefully and religiously observed. But as the Continental Congress are now sitting, who may probably appoint a fast for the same purpose, the Synod, from respect to that august body and for greater harmony with other denominations, and for the greater public order, if the Congress shall appoint a day not above four weeks distant from the said last Thursday of June, order that the congregations belonging to this Synod do keep the day appointed by Congress in obedience to this resolution; and if they appoint a day more distant, the Synod order both to be observed by all our communion. The Synod also earnestly recommend it to all the congregations under their care to spend the afternoon of the last Thursday in every month in public solemn prayer to God during the continuance of our present troubles."

This recommendation of the observance of a day for prayer every month was frequently repeated during the war.

Witherspoon, Rodgers and Caldwell were appointed a committee to perform the then unusual task of drawing up a pastoral letter to be sent to the churches.

"It bore throughout," says Dr. Gillett, "the stamp of their deep feeling and patriotic as well as religious zeal. Five hundred copies of this noble letter were ordered to be printed and circulated at the Synod's expense. Thus they were scattered throughout all the congregations, contributing in no small measure to kindle and sustain the patriotic zeal of the country."

"The Presbyterian Church, by act of its highest judicatory, thus took its stand at Philadelphia by the side of the American Congress, then in session, and its influence was felt in the most decisive manner throughout the bonds of the Church."

This pastoral letter thus begins:

"The Synod of New York and Philadelphia being met at a time when public affairs wear so threatening an aspect, and when, unless God in his sovereign providence speedily prevents it, all the horrors of a civil war throughout this great continent are to be apprehended, were of opinion that they could not discharge their duty to the numerous congregations under their care without addressing them at this important crisis. As the firm belief and habitual recollection of the power and presence of the living God ought at all times to possess the minds of real Christians, so in seasons of public calamity, when the Lord is known by the judgments which he executeth, it would be an ignorance or indifference highly criminal not to look up to him with reverence, to implore his mercy by humble and fervent prayer, and, if possible, to prevent his vengeance by timely repentance. We do, therefore, brethren, beseech you in the most earnest manner to look beyond the immediate authors either of your sufferings or fears, and to acknowledge the holiness and justice of the Almighty in the present visitation."

The Synod then exhorts the people to confession and repentance, reminding them that their prayers should be attended with a sincere purpose and through endeavor after personal and family reformation. "If thou prepare thine heart and stretch out thine hand toward him; if iniquity be in thine hands, put it far away, and let not wickedness dwell in thy tabernacles."

They considered it also a proper time to press on all of every rank seriously to consider the things which belong to their eternal peace, saying, "Hostilities long feared have now taken place; the sword has been drawn in one province, and the whole continent, with hardly any exception, seem determined to defend their rights by force of arms. If at the same time the British ministry shall continue to enforce their claims by violence, a lasting and bloody contest must be expected. Surely, then, it becomes those who have taken up arms and profess a willingness to hazard their lives in the cause of liberty to be prepared for death, which to many must be certain, and to every one is a possible or probable event.

"We have long seen with concern the circumstances which occasioned, and the gradual increase of, this unhappy difference. As ministers of the gospel of peace, we have ardently wished that it might be, and often hoped that it would have been, more early accommodated. It is well known to you, otherwise it would be imprudent indeed thus publicly to profess, that we have not been instrumental in inflaming the minds of the people or urging them to acts of violence and disorder. Perhaps no instance can be given on so interesting a subject in which political sentiments have been so long and so fully kept from the pulpit, and even malice itself has not charged us with laboring from the press. But things have now come to such a state that as we do not wish to conceal our opinions as men and citizens, so the relation in which we stand to you seemed to make the present improvement of it to your spiritual benefit an indispensable duty."

Then follows an exhortation directed principally to young men who might offer themselves as "champions of their country's cause" to cultivate piety, to reverence the name of God and to trust his providence. "The Lord is with you while ye be with him; and if ye seek him, he will be found of you: but if ye forsake him, he will forsake you."

After this exhortation the Synod offered special counsels to the churches as to their public and general conduct:

"First. In carrying on this important struggle, let every opportunity be taken to express your attachment and respect to our sovereign King George, and to the revolution principles by which his august family was seated on the British throne. We recommend, indeed, not only allegiance to him from principle and duty as the first magistrate of the empire, but esteem and reverence for the person of the prince, who has merited well of his subjects on many accounts, and who has probably been misled into his late and present measures by those about him; neither have we any doubt that they themselves have been in a great degree deceived by false representations from interested persons residing in America. It gives us the greatest pleasure to say, from our own certain knowledge of all belonging to our communion, and from the best means of information of far the greatest part of all denominations in this country, that the present opposition to the measures of administration does not in the least arise from disaffection to the king or a desire of separation from the parent State. We are happy in being able with truth to affirm that no part of America would either have approved or permitted such insults as have been offered to the sovereign in Great Britain. We exhort you, therefore, to continue in the same disposition, and not to suffer apprehension or injury itself easily to provoke you to anything which may seem to betray contrary sentiments. Let it ever appear that you only desire the preservation and security of those rights which belong to you as freemen and Britons, and that reconciliation upon these terms is your most ardent desire.

"Secondly. Be careful to maintain the union which at present subsists through the colonies. Nothing can be more manifest than that the success of every measure depends upon its being inviolably preserved, and therefore we hope you will leave nothing undone which can promote that end. In particular as the Continental Congress, now sitting at Philadelphia, consists of delegates chosen in the most free and unbiased manner by the body of the people, let them not only be treated with respect and encouraged in their difficult service, not only let your prayers be offered up to God for his direction in their proceedings, but adhere firmly to their resolutions, and let it be seen that they are able to bring out the whole strength of this vast country to carry them into execution. We would also advise for the same purpose that a spirit of candor, charity and mutual esteem be preserved and promoted toward those of different religious denominations. Persons of probity and principle of every profession should be united together as servants of the same Master; and the experience of our happy concord hitherto in a state of liberty should engage all to unite in support of the common interest; for there is no example in history in which civil liberty was destroyed and the rights of conscience preserved entire.

"Thirdly. We do earnestly exhort and beseech the societies under our care to be strict and vigilant in their private government, and to watch over the morals of their several members."

This duty is urged at some length, and then the letter proceeds thus:

"Fourthly. We cannot but recommend and urge in the warmest manner a regard to order and the public peace; and as in many places, during the confusion that prevails, legal proceedings have become difficult, it is hoped that all persons will conscientiously pay their just debts and to the utmost of their power serve one another, so that the evils inseparable from a civil war may not be augmented by wantonness and irregularity.

"Fifthly. We think it of importance at this time to recommend to all, of every rank, but especially to those who may be called to action, a spirit of humanity and mercy. Every battle of the warrior is with confused noise and garments rolled in blood. It is impossible to appeal to the sword without being exposed to many scenes of cruelty and slaughter, but it is often observed that civil wars are carried on with a rancor and spirit of revenge much greater than those between independent States. The injuries received or supposed in civil wars wound more deeply than those of foreign enemies. It is, therefore, more necessary to guard against this abuse, and recommend that meekness and gentleness of the spirit which is the noblest attendant on true valor. That man will fight most bravely who never begins to fight till it is necessary, and who ceases to fight as soon as the necessity is over.

"Lastly. We would recommend to all the societies under our care not to content themselves with attending devoutly on general fasts, but to continue habitually in the exercise of prayer, and to have frequent occasional voluntary meetings for solemn intercession with God on this important trial. Those who are immediately exposed to danger need your sympathy, and we learn from the Scriptures that fervency and importunity are the very characters of that prayer of the righteous man that availeth much. We conclude with our most earnest prayer that the God of heaven may bless you in your temporal and spiritual concerns, and that the present unnatural dispute may be speedily terminated by an equitable and lasting settlement on constitutional principles."

The Rev. Mr. Halsey, it is recorded, dissented from that paragraph of the above letter which contains the declarations of allegiance. This gentleman, it seems, was at least a year in advance, not only of the Synod, but of Congress. This pastoral letter contains a decided and unanimous expression on the part of the Synod of the side which it took in the great struggle for the liberties of America. It certainly does them and the Church which they represented great honor. They adhered to the last to the duties which they owed their sovereign; they approved of demanding no new liberties; they required only the secure possession of privileges which they were entitled to consider as their birthright.

The presbytery of Hanover, in a memorial presented to the legislature of Virginia in 1776, expressed with earnestness their hearty adoption of their country's cause. "Your memorialists," they say, "are governed by the same sentiments which have inspired the United States of America, and are determined that nothing in our power or influence shall be wanting to give success to their common cause. We would also represent that dissenters from the Church of England in this country have ever been desirous to conduct themselves as peaceable members of the civil government, for which reason they have hitherto submitted to several ecclesiastical burdens and restrictions that are inconsistent with equal liberty. But now, when the many and grievous oppressions of our mother-country have laid this continent under the necessity of casting off the yoke of tyranny and of forming independent governments upon equitable and liberal foundations, we flatter ourselves we shall be freed from all the encumbrances which a spirit of domination, prejudice or bigotry hath interwoven with our political systems. This we are the more strongly encouraged to expect by the Declaration of Rights, so universally applauded for that dignity, firmness and precision with which it delineates and asserts the privileges of society and the prerogatives of human nature, and which we embrace as the magna charta of our commonwealth, that can never be violated without endangering the grand superstructure it was destined to sustain."

As at the beginning, so also at the close, of the war, the Synod directed a pastoral letter to their congregations expressing their sentiments in relation to the contest. In the letter written in 1783 they say:

"We cannot help congratulating you on the general and almost universal attachment of the Presbyterian body to the cause of liberty and the rights of mankind. This has been visible in their conduct, and has been confessed by the complaints and resentment of the common enemy. Such a circumstance ought not only to afford us satisfaction on the review as bringing credit to the body in general, but to increase our gratitude to God for the happy issue of the war. Had it been unsuccessful, we must have drunk deeply of the cup of suffering. Our burnt and wasted churches and our plundered dwellings in such places as fell under the power of our adversaries are but an earnest of what we must have suffered had they finally prevailed.

"The Synod therefore requests you to render thanks to almighty God for all his mercies, spiritual and temporal, and in a particular manner for establishing the independence of the United States of America. He is the supreme Disposer, and to him belongs the glory, the victory and the majesty. We are persuaded you will easily recollect many circumstances in the course of the struggle which point out his special and signal interposition in our favor. Our most remarkable successes have generally been when things had just before worn the most unfavorable aspect, as at Trenton and Saratoga at the beginning, in South Carolina and Virginia toward the end, of the war. They specify, among other mercies, the assistance derived from France and the happy selection 'of a commander-in-chief of the armies of the United States, who in this important and difficult charge has given universal satisfaction, who was alike acceptable to the citizen and the soldier, to the State in which he was born and to every other on the continent, and whose character and influence, after so long service, are not only unimpaired but augmented.'"

On the election of Washington to the presidency, the General Assembly appointed a committee to prepare an address of congratulation, which was as follows:

"SIR: The General Assembly of the Presbyterian Church in the United States of America embrace the earliest opportunity in their power to testify the lively and unfeigned pleasure which they, with the rest of their fellow-citizens, feel on your appointment to the first office in the nation.

"We adore almighty God, the author of every perfect gift, who hath endued you with such a rare and happy assemblage of talents as hath rendered you equally necessary to your country in war and in peace. Your military achievements ensured safety and glory to America in the late arduous conflict for freedom, while your disinterested conduct and uniformly just disinterested of the public interest gained you the entire confidence of the people; and in the present interesting period of public affairs the influence of your personal character moderates the divisions of political parties and promises a permanent establishment of the civil government.

"From a retirement more glorious than thrones and sceptres you have been called to your present elevated station by the voice of a great and free people, and with an unanimity of suffrage that has few, if any, examples in history. A man more ambitious of fame or less devoted to his country would have refused an office in which his honors could not be augmented, and where they might possibly be subject to a reverse. We are happy that God has inclined your heart to give yourself once more to the public. And we derive a favorable presage of the event from the zeal of all classes of the people and their confidence in your virtues, as well as from the knowledge and dignity with which the Federal councils are filled. But we derive a presage even more flattering from the piety of your character. Public virtue is the most certain means of public felicity, and religion is the surest basis of virtue. We therefore esteem it a peculiar happiness to behold in our chief magistrate a steady, uniform, avowed friend of the Christian religion, who has commenced his administration in rational and exalted sentiments of piety, and who, in his private conduct, adorns the doctrines of the gospel of Christ, and on the most public and solemn occasions devoutly acknowledges the government of divine Providence.

"The example of distinguished characters will ever possess a powerful and extensive influence on the public mind. And when we see in such a conspicuous station the amiable example of piety to God, of benevolence to men and of a pure and virtuous patriotism, we naturally hope that it will diffuse its influence, and that eventually the most happy consequences will result from it. To the force of imitation we will endeavor to add the wholesome instructions of religion. We shall consider ourselves as doing an acceptable service to God in our profession when we contribute to render men sober, honest and industrious citizens, and the obedient subjects of a lawful government. In these pious labors we hope to imitate the most worthy of our brethren of other Christian denominations, and to be imitated by them, assured that is we can by mutual and generous emulation promote truth and virtue, we shall render a great and important service to the republic—shall receive encouragement from every wise and good citizen, and, above all, meet the approbation of our divine Master.

"We pray almighty God to have you always in his holy keeping. May he prolong your valuable life, an ornament and a blessing to your country, and at last bestow on you the glorious reward of a faithful servant!"

To which Washington replied:

*"To the General Assembly of the Presbyterian Church in the United States of America.*

"GENTLEMAN: I received with great sensibility the testimonial given by the General Assembly of the Presbyterian Church in the United States of America of the lively and unfeigned pleasure experienced by them on my appointment to the first office in the nation.

"Although it will be my endeavor to avoid being elated by the too favorable opinion which your kindness for me many have induced you to express of the importance of my former conduct and the effect of my future services, yet, conscious of the disinterestedness of my motives, it is not necessary for me to conceal the satisfaction I have felt upon finding that my compliance with the call of my country and my dependence on the assistance of Heaven to support me in my arduous undertaking have, so far as I can learn, met the universal approbation of my countrymen. While I reiterate the professions of my dependence upon Heaven as the source of all public and private blessings, I will observe that the general prevalence of piety,

GEORGE WASHINGTON

"WHILE ALL MEN WITHIN OUR TERRITORIES ARE PROTECTED IN WORSHIPING THE DEITY ACCORDING TO THE DICTATES OF THEIR CONSCIENCES, IT IS RATIONALLY TO BE EXPECTED FROM THEM IN RETURN THAT THEY WILL ALL BE EMULOUS OF EVINCING THE SINCERITY OF THEIR PROFESSIONS BY THE INNOCENCE OF THEIR LIVES AND THE BENEVOLENCE OF THEIR ACTIONS. FOR NO MAN WHO IS PROFLIGATE IN HIS MORALS OR A BAD MEMBER OF THE CIVIL COMMUNITY CAN POSSIBLY BE A TRUE CHRISTIAN OR A CREDIT TO THIS OWN RELIGIOUS SOCIETY."

philanthropy, honestly, industry and economy seems, in the ordinary course of human affairs, particularly necessary for advancing and confirming the happiness of our country. While all men within our territories are protected in worshiping the Deity according to the dictates of their consciences, it is rationally to be expected from them in return that they will all be emulous of evincing the sincerity of their professions by the innocence of their lives and the benevolence of their actions. For no man who is profligate in his morals or a bad member of the civil community can possibly be a true Christian or a credit to his own religious society.

"I desire you to accept my acknowledgements for your laudable endeavors to render men sober, honest and good citizens, and the obedient subjects of a lawful government, as well as for your prayers to almighty God for his blessings on our common country and the instrument which he has been pleased to make use of in the administration of its government.*

"GEORGE WASHINGTON."

*The original of this letter is in the possession of the Presbyterian Board of Publication, Philadelphia.

# 9

# Declaration of Independence and Dr. John Witherspoon

The services of Presbyterianism in the cause of American liberty present two points of special and commanding interest, the one concerning the Declaration of Independence, the other concerning the organization of the national confederacy.

The Reading of the Declaration of Independence

We are apt to think that the Declaration of Independence was so completely a matter of course that there could have been neither question as to its propriety nor opposition to it except from enemies to the patriot cause. In truth, however, the subject was hedged about with difficulties numerous and great. Even for a full year after the martyrs had fallen at Lexington, Concord and Breed's Hill (we venture to give the true name in this last case, as it is well known that neither was the battle fought, nor does the monument stand, on Bunker Hill), vast numbers of true-hearted patriots shrank from the thought of severance from the mother-country as a true son shrinks from renouncing connection with his parental home.

Yet on the 17th of May, 1776, kept as a national fast, Mr. Bancroft tells us that "George Duffield, the minister of the Third Presbyterian Church in Philadelphia, with John Adams for a listener, drew a parallel between George III and Pharaoh, and inferred that the same providence of God which had rescued the Israelites intended to free the Americans."

Whoever hesitated, Presbyterians did not. On the day this sermon was preached the provincial assembly of Pennsylvania voted to leave the question of independence to the direction of their delegates in Congress, knowing that a majority of those delegates were *opposed* to independence, Dickinson pledging his word that they would vote against the measure. The next day the most copious and animated debate ever held upon the subject took place in Congress, lasting from ten in the morning till seven in the evening, Robert Livingston of New York, Wilson, Dickinson and Edward Rutledge *ardently opposing* it.

On Monday the 10th of June, Rutledge moved that the question be postponed for three weeks, and it is significant of the state of feeling that this motion, after a whole day's discussion, was carried.

The next day a committee of five, with Jefferson at its head, was appointed to prepare a formal Declaration of Independence and report it to the House.

On Friday the 28th of June, the delegation from the provincial Congress of New Jersey appeared in Congress, and among them the *only clergyman* that sat in that body, *Dr. John Witherspoon,* Presbyterian minister and president of the College of New Jersey.

Of Dr. Witherspoon, Mr. Bancroft writes in the sixth chapter of his history:

"In New Jersey, Witherspoon, a Presbyterian minister and *'as high a Son of Liberty as any in America,'* met the committee at new Brunswick in July, 1774, and with William Livingston, member of the Presbyterian congregation of Elizabeth, New Jersey, labored to instruct their delegates that the tea should not be paid for."

Also, in his sixty-seventh chapter: "The new provincial Congress of New Jersey, which came fresh from the people with ample powers, and organized itself on the evening of the 11th of June, 1776, was opened with prayer by John Witherspoon, an eloquent Scottish minister of the same faith with John Knox, a man of great ability, learning and liberality, ready to dash into pieces all false gods. Born near Edinburgh, trained up at its university, in 1768 he removed to Princeton to become the successor of Jonathan Edwards, Davies and Finley as president of its college. A combatant of skepticism and the narrow philosophy of the materialists, he was deputed by Somerset county to take part in applying his noble theories to the construction of a civil government."

A lineal descendant of John Knox, he was born in Haddingtonshire, Scotland, February 5, 1722; ordained to the ministry in 1745; became president of the College of New Jersey in 1768; died near Princeton, September 15, 1794. He comes before us in history as a "many-sided man." A scholar of the largest culture, a profound theologian, a faithful and laborious pastor, an orator of commanding eloquence, a successful teacher, a voluminous and successful author, a skillful financier and a great leader among men—it is difficult to say in which of these characters he shone to most advantage. By birth and training the adversary of wrong and oppression in whatever form, immediately on his arrival in this country he identified himself with the colonial cause. Grasping, as by intuition, the great principles involved in the struggle with the mother-country, his powerful advocacy of American rights speedily elevated him to his proper place by the side of Hancock, Jefferson, Franklin and their illustrious compeers.

As a member of the convention that formed the constitution of New Jersey, Dr. Witherspoon astonished and impressed his coadjutors by his knowledge and wisdom as a civilian.

For six years he was a member of the Continental Congress, for the duties of which position "he was eminently qualified not only by the clearness and vigor of his intellect, the calmness of his judgment and his indomitable strength of purpose, but by an uncommon familiarity with the forms of public business, acquired from the position which he held as a leader in the church courts in his native country." The value of his services in that body cannot be overestimated, and the extent and weight of his influence on the country was immeasurable.

Sanderson, in his *Biography of the Signers of the Declaration*, writes:

"It is impossible to specify the numerous services in which he was engaged during his long continuance in Congress.

"His talents as a politician had been thoroughly tested previous to his emigration, as leader of the orthodox party in the Church of Scotland; and he was fully prepared to play a much more important part on the theatre of our grand Revolution than by displaying his eloquence and sagacity in the Presbyteries, Synods and General Assemblies of Scotland."

The firm and united adherence to Washington and his cause of the large Scotch and Scotch-Irish population was due in no small degree to their confidence in their piety, ability and wisdom of Dr. Witherspoon.

He was a member of "the secret committee" of Congress, whose duties were of the first importance in the prosecution of the war.

In November, 1776, when the army was on the eve of dissolution and all hearts were lapsing into despair, Dr. Witherspoon and two others were appointed a committee to visit and confer with Washington on the condition of affairs.

In December, when Congress had been driven from Philadelphia to Baltimore, Dr. Witherspoon, Richard Henry Lee and John Adams, having been appointed a committee for the purpose, issued a heart-stirring appeal to the people. Dr. Witherspoon was an active and very efficient member of the "Board of War."

In 1778 he was appointed, with three others, to prepare a manifesto on the brutal treatment by the British of American prisoners, and the eloquent and touching paper reported by this committee was adopted by a unanimous vote of Congress.

The same year he was appointed, with Robert Morris, Elbridge Gerry, Richard Henry Lee and Gouverneur Morris, a committee upon the finances.

In 1779 he greatly distinguished himself as a member of the committee to secure supplies for the famishing army.

The same year, when a body of people residing within the "New Hampshire Grants" insisted upon establishing themselves as an independent State, giving rise to great confusion and bitter animosities, Dr. Witherspoon, with four others, was appointed a committee to conduct the delicate negotiations involved in this perplexing matter.

In the superlatively important financial questions that harassed and imperiled the infant republic, the adjustment of which "saved the country and exalted a Morris to the rank and grandeur of a Washington," Witherspoon was, more than any other man, the trusted counselor of the great financier.

Through the darkest hour of the war his courage was conspicuous and his resolution indomitable. When, after the defeat on Long Island, Lord Howe's propositions came before Congress, Mr. Bancroft says:

"Witherspoon, with a very great majority of the members, looked upon them as an insult."

Like Rush and Witherspoon, John Adams spoke vehemently against the proposed conference.

Again Bancroft writes: "It was from Witherspoon of New Jersey that Madison, bred in the school of Presbyterian dissenters under Witherspoon at Princeton, imbibed the lesson of perfect freedom in matters of conscience. When the constitution of that State was framed by a convention composed chiefly of Presbyterians, they established perfect liberty of conscience without the blemish of a test."

On the 17$^{th}$ of May, 1776, appointed by Congress as a general fast day, Dr. Witherspoon preached a sermon, in which he said:

"It would be criminal not to observe the interposition of Providence in American affairs. Some important victories have been gained with so little loss that enemies will probably think it has been dissembled. The signal advantage gained by the evacuation of Boston and the shameful flight of the army and navy of Britain was brought about without the loss of a man.

"I willingly embrace the opportunity of declaring my opinion that the cause in which America is now in arms is the cause of justice, liberty and human nature.

"Everybody must perceive the absolute necessity of union.

"He is the best friend of American liberty who is most sincere and active in promoting true and undefiled religion. An avowed enemy to God I scruple not to call an enemy to his country. I do not wish you to oppose any man's religion, but everybody's wickedness. The cause is sacred, and its champions should be holy.

"I exhort all who go not to the field to apply themselves with the utmost diligence to works of industry. It is in your power by this means not only to supply the necessities, but to add strength to your country.

"Suffer me to recommend to you frugality in your families and every other article of expense. Temperance in meals, moderation and decency in dress, furniture and equipage have, I think, generally been characteristics of a distinguished patriot.

"God grant that in America true religion and civil liberty may be inseparable, and that the unjust attempts to destroy the one may in the issue tend to the support and establishment of the other."

This sermon was published and dedicated to "The Hon. John Hancock, Esq., President of the Congress of the United States of America." To the sermon was appended an "Address to the natives of Scotland residing in America." Of this sermon and address a writer in a recent number of the *New York Evangelist* says:

"This sermon was printed in Philadelphia and reprinted the next year at Glasgow. The object of the editors in thus reproducing it was openly avowed in their preface. It was 'to show what artful means and fallacious arguments have been made use of by ambitious and self-designing men to stir up the poor infatuated Americans to the present rebellious measures—what an active hand even Dr. Witherspoon has had therein—to convince his friends in this country of the truth of his being a chief promoter of the American revolt, and that, if he falls into the hands of government and meets with the demerit of his offence, he hath justly and deservedly procured it to himself.'

"In an appendix to the sermon it was added to his discredit—although what was then a reproach to his name has now become an honor to his memory—that 'the scheme of independency, it is said, was first planned by him, and success to the independent States of America, we are told, was a favorite toast at the doctor's table when entertaining a number of delegates before it was resolved on by the Congress.'

"The language of the editor of the Scottish edition of the sermon reflects the bitterness with which the name of Dr. Witherspoon was mentioned in Scotland. He went forth from his native land almost an exile, virtually ostracized by that 'moderatism' in the Church which he had so scathingly exposed and so keenly ridiculed in his 'Characteristics.'

"We may add that for the facts which we have here given we are indebted to a copy of the Scotch edition of Dr. Witherspoon's sermon, Glasgow, 1777, belonging to the library of D.H. McAlpin of this city."

Conspicuous among the claims of Witherspoon upon the grateful applause of the nation is the fullness of his confidence in Washington, and the uncompromising fidelity of his adherence to him through evil report and good report. This merit is the more conspicuous as it contrasts so strongly with the lukewarmness, and even distrust and opposition, of not a few in the Continental Congress, whose course at various times during the war made the great heart of Washington to ache and put the country's cause in jeopardy.

In Bancroft's fourteenth chapter we read:

"In Congress, which had become distracted by selfish schemes, there were signs of impatience at his (Washington's) superiority, and an obstinate reluctance to own that the depressed condition of the country was due to their having refused to heed his advice. In a proposition for giving him the power to remove generals, John Adams objected vehemently, saying: 'In private life I am willing to respect and look up to him; in the house I feel myself to be the superior of General Washington.'

"Washington was surrounded by officers willing to fill the ears of members of Congress with clamor against his management or opinions in counteraction of his advice.

"With unselfish and untiring zeal, Washington strove to repair the errors and defects of Congress. From the weakness of its powers it would justly escape reprehension if its members had unanimously given him their support, but some of them indulged in open expressions of discontent.

"Assuming the style of conquerors, they did not, and would not, perceive the true situation of affairs. They were vexed that the commander-in-chief insisted on bringing it to their attention; and as if Washington had not adventured miracles of daring, Samuel Adams and others were habitually impatient for more enterprise.

"Washington bore their unjust reproaches with meekness and dignity, never forgetting the obedience and respect that were due to Congress as his civil superior and the representative of all the States."

Now, while even patriots like Samuel and John Adams, to say nothing of men of lower grade, were misled to censure where they should have applauded, it is something well worthy of observation and admiration that Witherspoon was always on the side of the Father of his Country.

Not least prominent among the features of Dr. Witherspoon's character was his masculine and decided piety.

"His personal religion," writes one, "is well known. Few men were ever more anxious to walk close with God, and by a solid, righteous and pious life to adorn the doctrine of the gospel. Besides the daily devotions of the closet and the family, he regularly set apart with his household the last day of every year for fasting, humiliation and prayer. He was also in the practice of spending days in secret exercises of this kind as occasion required."

As to his theology, we hardly need the assurance that "it was Calvinistic according to the system of Calvin himself, subject only to the modification which it has received in the standards of the Presbyterian Church. Between him and Calvin, indeed, there was in talents and improvements no inconsiderable resemblance. Both were men of great intellectual powers, both eminent divines, both distinguished heads of literary institutions, both erudite civilians and both keen satirists. Dr. Witherspoon certainly possessed a peculiar talent for presenting the Calvinistic doctrines in a popular form, and in a manner the least offensive to those who do not hold them, while he maintained them firmly in their substance."

Of Witherspoon, Dr. Ashbel Green writes:

DR. ASHBEL GREEN

"In person Dr. Witherspoon was of the middle size. He was fleshy, with a tendency to corpulence. His limbs were well proportioned and his complexion fair. His eyes were strongly indicative of intelligence. His eyebrows were large, hanging down at the ends next his temples. His countenance united gravity with benignity in its general expression. The features of his face possessed much of what painters denominate character, and of course he was a good subject for the pencil. His public appearance was always graceful and venerable, and in promiscuous company he had more of the quality called *presence* than any other individual with whom the writer has ever had intercourse, Washington excepted.

"Dr. Witherspoon was a man of genius. His chief mental strength lay in his reasoning faculty. He was a powerful thinker. When he took hold of a subject, he searched it to the bottom, and in discussing it he often treated it analytically and synthetically. It was surprising to observe with what readiness he could see through a complicated and perplexed subject, estimate its real merits and bearing, disentangle it and present it in its true aspect."

At length the three weeks through which action on the resolution on Independence was postponed draw to a close. On Friday, June 28, Witherspoon and the other New Jersey delegates take their seat in Congress. The resolution comes up, and a further postponement is suggested to enable the newly-arrived members to become more

Dr. John Witherspoon

DR. WITHERSPOON WAS A MAN OF GENIUS. HIS CHIEF MENTAL STRENGTH LAY IN HIS REASONING FACULTY. HE WAS A POWERFUL THINKER. WHEN HE TOOK HOLD OF A SUBJECT, HE SEARCHED IT TO THE BOTTOM, AND IN DISCUSSING IT HE OFTEN TREATED IT ANALYTICALLY AND SYNTHETICALLY.

familiar with the momentous matter in hand. To this suggestion Dr. Witherspoon answered that for one he was no stranger to the subject, and that he was ready for action. To the suggestion that the colonies were not ripe for the measure he answered that in his judgment "they were rotting for the want of it."

The motion was carried that on Monday, July the first, the House go into a committee of the whole upon the subject. Monday came, and fifty members were in their seats. They sat, as usual, with closed doors. The committee on the Declaration had made their report, and that report lay on the table. All that day the resolution was debated, and at the close nine colonies voted for it. South Carolina and Pennsylvania voted unanimously against, and Delaware was divided.

On Tuesday the House again went into committee of the whole, and the discussion was continued, and at the close twelve colonies voted for it, New York not voting. A day intervened, and on Thursday, at the close of the day, the same twelve colonies passed the Declaration of Independence, New York assenting afterward. During the debates of these four momentous days the measure encountered strenuous opposition. Dickenson, of Pennsylvania, one of the most respected and one of the ablest members of the House, opposed the measure in a protracted and elaborate argument.

Of the following synopsis of Mr. Dickinson's argument Mr. Bancroft says: "It is from a report made by himself that I abridge his elaborate discourse, using no words but his own.

"'I value the love of my country,' said Mr. Dickinson, 'as I ought, but I value my country more; and I desire this illustrious assembly to witness the integrity, if not the policy, of my conduct. The first campaign will be decisive of the controversy. The Declaration will not strengthen us by one man or by the least supply, while it may expose our soldiers to additional cruelties.

"'No instance is recollected of a people, without a battle fought or an ally gained, abrogating for ever their connection with a warlike commercial empire. It might unite the different parties in Great Britain against us, and create disunion among ourselves.

"'With other powers it would rather injure than avail us. Foreign aid will not be obtained but by our actions in the field, which are the only evidences of our union and vigor that will be respected. In the war between the United Provinces and Spain, France and England assisted the provinces before they declared themselves independent. If it is the interest of any European kingdom to aid us, we shall be aided without such a Declaration; if it is not, we shall be aided with it.

"'Before such an irrevocable step shall be taken, we ought to know the disposition of the great powers, and how far they will permit any one or more of them to interfere.

"'The erection of an independent empire on this continent is a phenomenon in the world. Its effects will be immense, and may vibrate round the globe. How they may affect or any be supposed to affect old establishments is not ascertained.

"'It is singularly disrespectful to France to make the declaration before her sense is known, as we have sent an agent expressly to inquire whether such a declaration would be acceptable to her, and we have reason to believe he is now arrived at the court of Versailles. The measure ought to be delayed till the common interest shall in the best manner be consulted by common consent.

"'Besides, the door to accommodation with Great Britain ought not to be shut until we know what terms can be obtained from some competent power. Thus to break with her before we have compacted with another is to make experiments on the lives and liberties of my countrymen, which I would sooner die than agree to make. At best, it is to throw us into the hands of some other power and to lie at its mercy, for we shall have passed the river that is never to be repassed. We ought to retain the declaration, and remain masters of our own fame and fate. We ought to inform that power that we are filled with a just detestation of our oppressors—that we are determined to cast off for ever all subjection to them, and to declare ourselves independent, and to support that declaration with our lives and fortunes, provided that power will approve the proceeding, acknowledge our independence and enter into a treaty with us upon equitable and advantageous conditions.

"'Other objections to the Declaration at this time are suggested by our internal circumstances. The formation of our government and an agreement upon the terms of our confederation ought to precede the assumption of our station among sovereigns. A sovereignty composed of several distinct bodies of men not subject to established constitutions, and not combined together by confirmed articles of union, is such a sovereignty as has never appeared. These particulars would not be unobserved by foreign kingdoms and States, and they will wait for other proofs of political energy before they will treat us with the desired attention.

"'With respect to ourselves the consideration is still more serious. The forming of our government is a new and difficult work. When this is done, and the people perceive that they and their posterity are to live under well-regulated constitutions, they will be encouraged to look forward to independence as completing the noble system of their political happiness. The objects nearest to them are now enveloped in clouds, and those more distant appear confused. The relation one citizen is to bear to another, and the connection one State is to have with another, they do not, cannot, know. Mankind are naturally attached to plans of government that promise quiet and security. General satisfaction with them when formed would, indeed, be a great point attained; but persons of reflection will perhaps think it absolutely necessary that Congress should institute some mode for preserving them from future discords.

"'The confederation ought to be settled before the declaration of independence. Foreigners will think it most regular. The weaker States will not be in so much danger of having disadvantageous terms imposed upon them by the stronger. If the Declaration is first made, political necessities may urge on the acceptance of conditions highly disagreeable to parts of the Union. The present comparative circumstances of the colonies are now tolerably well understood. But some have very extraordinary claims to territory, which, if admitted, as they might be in a future confederation, the terms of it not being yet adjusted, all idea of the present comparisons between them would be confounded. Those whose boundaries are acknowledged would sink in proportion to the elevation of their neighbors.

"'Besides, the unlocated lands not comprehended within acknowledged boundaries are deemed a fund sufficient to defray a vast part, if not the whole, of the expenses of the war. These ought to be considered as the property of all, acquired by the arms of all. For these reasons the boundaries of the colonies ought to be fixed before the declaration, and their respective rights mutually guaranteed; and the unlocated lands ought also, previous to that declaration, to be solemnly appropriated to the benefit of all, for it may be extremely difficult, if not impracticable, to obtain these decisions afterward.

"'Upon the whole, when things shall thus be deliberately rendered firm at home and favorable abroad, then let America, *Attolens humeris famam et fata nepotum*—bearing upon her shoulders glory and the destiny of her descendants—advance with majestic steps

He was honored for spotless morals, eloquence and good service in the colonial legislature, and his writings hand endeared him to America as a sincere friend of liberty. He had an excellent heart, and the cause of his country lay near it.

John Dickinson

and assume her station among the sovereigns of the world.'"

Now, when we consider the character and ability of the man who spoke these words, and ponder well the words themselves, we shall feel that together they must have carried with them a prodigious weight.

John Dickinson, "the illustrious farmer" of Pennsylvania, was one who "had been taught from infancy to love humanity and liberty." His claims to public respect all acknowledged. "He was honored for spotless morals, eloquence and good service in the colonial legislature, and his writings had endeared him to America as a sincere friend of liberty. He had an excellent heart, and the cause of his country lay near it."

In 1767 he had written sentences that rang through all the colonies. Respecting the British scheme of taxation, he wrote: "This is an *innovation,* and a most dangerous innovation. We being obliged to take commodities from Great Britain, special duties on their exportation to us are as much taxes upon us as those imposed by the Stamp Act. We are in the situation of a besieged city surrounded in every part but one. If that is closed up, no step can be taken but to surrender at discretion.

"I would persuade the people of these colonies immediately, vigorously and unanimously to exert themselves in the most firm but the most peaceable manner for obtaining relief. If an inveterate resolution is formed to annihilate the liberties of the governed, English history affords examples of resistance by force."

Thus wrote this able, wise and pure patriot in 1767; nor was his patriotism any the less above question in 1776.

Besides, if we recall to mind the circumstances of the hour, we can see that in many ears his words had the ring of the soundest wisdom, and can realize in some degree the heroic intrepidity and indomitable resolution required in those who took the opposite view and urged to immediate action.

But in behalf of the Declaration, Adams thundered like a Demosthenes and Witherspoon pleaded like a Cicero.

"When the Declaration of Independence was under debate"—we quote the words of the Rev. Dr. John M. Krebs, of New York—"doubts and forebodings were whispered through the hall. The House hesitated, wavered, and for a while liberty and slavery appeared to hang in even scale. It was then that an aged patriarch arose—a venerable and stately form, his head white with the frost of years.

"Every eye went to him with the quickness of thought and remained with the fixedness of the polar star. He cast on the assembly a look of inexpressible interest and unconquerable determination, while on his visage the hue of age was lost in the flush of burning patriotism that fired his cheek.

"'There is,' said he, 'a tide in the affairs of men, a nick of time. We perceive it now before us. To hesitate is to consent to our own slavery. That noble instrument upon your table, which ensures immortality to its author, should be subscribed this very morning by every pen in this house. He that will not respond to its accents and strain every nerve to carry into effect its provisions is unworthy the name of freeman.

"'For my own part, of property I have some, of reputation more. That reputation is staked, that property is pledged, on the issue of this contest; and although these gray hairs must soon descend into the sepulcher, I would infinitely rather that they descend thither by the hand of the executioner than desert at this crisis the sacred cause of my country.'"

"Witherspoon, of New Jersey," says Mr. Bancroft, "urged that the country was fully ripe for the great decision, and that delay alone was fraught with peril."

# 10

# Organization of the Confederacy

Next in importance to the Declaration was the organization of the colonies into a confederacy. Independence of Great Britain might be secured by victory in the field, and yet little but confusion and oft-recurring and protracted intestine conflict ensue, unless the isolated States were drawn together into a harmonious and compact national Union.

Judge Story, in his fourth chapter on *The Constitution*, writes: "The union of the colonies during the Revolution 'grew out of the exigencies and dangers of the times, and would naturally terminate with the return of peace.'

"As little could it escape observation how great would be the dangers of the separation of the confederated States into independent communities, acknowledging no common head and acting upon no common system. Rivalries, jealousies, real or imaginary wrongs, diversities of local interests and institutions, would soon sever the ties of a common attachment which bound them together, and bring on a state of hostile operations dangerous to their peace and subversive of their permanent interests."

At this late day it is not unnatural to assume that the organization of a permanent confederation was as easy as the need of it was obvious. And yet the fact is that so many and obstinate were the difficulties that stood in the way that from the time when Franklin first made the motion for it in Congress to the time when the confederacy was actually organized, more than five long years passed away. And it was more than sixteen months after Congress appointed a committee consisting of one member from each colony to digest a plan for a confederation before Congress adopted a plan and by vote submitted it to the colonies for their assent. And then four years more elapsed before the assent of the colonies could be secured.

The difficulties that impeded the formation of a confederate union were clearly set forth in the circular transmitted with the articles as adopted by Congress to the several State legislatures. In this circular Congress thus excuses itself for apparent tardiness in the matter: "To form a permanent union accommodated to the opinions and wishes of the delegates of so many States differing in habits, produce, commerce and internal police was found to be a work which nothing but time and reflection, conspiring with a disposition to conciliate, could mature and accomplish."

The main hindrance to the formation of a Federal Union centered around the reluctance of the several States to yield to a general government any of the powers they possessed.

"There was not," writes Mr. Bancroft, "at that time one single statesman who fully comprehended the need of the country."

We more than suspect that there were at least *one* exception to this sweeping remark. Still, at that time "each one of the colonies connected its idea of freedom and safety with the exclusive privilege of managing its internal policy. And they delighted to keep fresh the proud memories of repeated victories won over the persistent attempt of the agents of a supreme power which was external to themselves to impose restrictions on their domestic autonomy."

Edward Rutledge, of South Carolina, "saw danger in the *very thought* of an indissoluble league of friendship between the States for their general welfare." And of even the little less than anarchical scheme proposed in Congress in July, 1776, he said: "If it be adopted, nothing less than ruin to some colonies will be the consequence."

It is no wonder, therefore, that we read that "seemingly irreconcilable differences of opinion left Congress no heart to continue the work of confederation."

For sixteen months from the report of a plan of confederation "the spirit of separation fostered by opposing interests," dread of interference of one State in the affairs of another, fears on the part of the South of the more compact and homogeneous North, "*visibly increased* in Congress."

Each colony retained a traditional jealousy of any interference from without with its internal privileges. As they had forbidden king and parliament, so now they forbade any confederate government, to levy taxes or duties except for postage. The relation of slaves to freeman in the basis of representation formed another vexing question. Another, not less troublesome, was whether the smaller States should have equal vote in the Congress with the larger ones. And as arduous as any other problem was that involved in the conflicting claims to the vast territories of western lands. New Hampshire and five or six other States had boundaries well defined. But other of the colonies extended, according to their charters, to the Mississippi, or even to the Pacific Ocean. The former insisted that this vast western domain ought to be a joint property, while the latter claimed each its own share for its own purposes as a source of revenue. On this point Judge Story writes:

"This subject was one of a perpetually recurring and increasing irritation, and the confederation would never have been acceded to if Virginia and New York had not at last consented to make liberal cessions of the territory within their respective boundaries for national purposes."

Thus years rolled away ere a confederation became possible.

Now, a point on which Presbyterians love to dwell is the inherent tendency of their system toward *organization*. Just as naturally as the seed germinates Presbyterianism organizes. It is itself an organism; and if Nature abhors a vacuum, Presbyterianism abhors disintegration or anything that tends thereto.

"Everything organic," writes Dr. Charles Hodge, "has what may be called a *nisus formatives*, an inward force by which it is impelled to assume the form suited to its nature."

CHARLES HODGE

THUS PRESBYTERIANISM IS NOT AN EXTERNAL FRAMEWORK. IT IS A REAL GROWTH. IT IS THE OUTWARD EXPRESSION OF AN INWARD LAW. A SCORE OF PRESBYTERIANS, SHIPWRECKED IN HELPLESS EXILE UPON A DISTANT SHORE, WOULD AS CERTAINLY ORGANIZE BY THE ELECTION OF A PASTORY AND A BODY OF ELDERS TO RULE THEM AS THE SUN IS SURE TO RISE IN THE MORNING.

Thus Presbyterianism "is not an external framework. It is a real growth. It is the outward expression of an inward law." A score of Presbyterians, shipwrecked in helpless exile upon a distant shore, would as certainly organize by the election of a pastor and a body of elders to rule them as the sun is sure to rise in the morning. Possessed of this spirit, it is the most natural thing in the world that Presbyterianism should demand order and organization wherever practicable in all with which it has to do. And Dr. Witherspoon being a Presbyterian from the crown of his head to the sole of his foot, it was one of the most natural things in the world that he, when the subject of organizing the chaos of independent States into a compact system of order and subordination came before Congress, should at once see its necessity, believe in its practicability, and throw all the energy of his nature into the effort for its realization. Accordingly, in Saunderson's *Lives of the Signers of the Declaration* we read:

"Dr. Witherspoon warmly maintained the absolute necessity of union to impart vigor and success to the measures of government, and he *strongly combated* the opinion expressed in Congress that a lasting confederacy among the States was impracticable. He declared that such sentiments were calculated greatly to depress the minds of the people and weaken their efforts in defence of the country.

"'I confess,' said he, 'such a conviction would to me greatly diminish the glory and importance of the struggle, whether considered as for the rights of mankind in general, or for the prosperity and happiness of this continent in future times. It would quite depreciate the object of hope, as well as place it at a greater distance.

"'For what would it signify to risk our possessions and shed our blood to set ourselves free from the encroachments and oppressions of Great Britain, with a certainty, as soon as peace was settled with them, of a more lasting war, a more unnatural, a more bloody and much more hopeless war among the colonies themselves?

"'If, at present, when the danger is yet imminent, when it is so far from being over that it is but coming to its height, we shall find it impossible to agree upon the terms of this confederacy, what madness is it to suppose that there ever will be a time or that circumstances will so change as to make it even probable that it will be done at an after season! Will not the very same difficulties that are in our way be in the way of those who shall come after us? Is it possible that they should be ignorant of or inattentive to them?

Will they not have the same jealousies of each other, the same attachment to local prejudices or particular interests? So certain is this that I look upon delay here as in the repentance of a sinner, though it adds to the necessity yet augments the difficulty and takes away from the inclination.'"

A sentiment expressed in this debate that it was to be expected from the nature of men that a time must come when a confederacy would be dissolved and broken in pieces, and which seemed to create an indifference as to the success of the measure, produced the following burst of eloquence:

"I am none of those who either deny or conceal the depravity of human nature till it is purified by the light of truth and renewed by the Spirit of the living God. Yet I apprehend there is no force in that reasoning at all. Shall we establish nothing good because we know it cannot be eternal? Shall we live without government because every constitution has its old age and its period? Because we know that we shall die, shall we take no pains to preserve or lengthen our life? Far from it, sir. It only requires the more watchful attention to settle the government on the best principles and in the wisest manner, that it may last as long as the nature of things will admit."

Dr. Witherspoon concluded his eloquent arguments in favor of a well-planned confederation in the following terms:

"For all these reasons, sir, I humbly apprehend that every argument from honor, interest, safety and necessity conspires in pressing us to a confederacy; and if it be seriously attempted, I hope, by the blessing of God upon our endeavors, it will be happily accomplished."

Grouping together, then, these facts among others—the fact that Presbyterianism is in its own nature a system of pure representative republican government, and as such in striking harmony, both in form and spirit, with that of the State and nation; that it has always been peculiarly odious to tyrants; the numerous patriotic deliverances of the Synod of New York and Philadelphia and of some of the Presbyteries of our Church; the fact that "the first voice publicly raised in America to dissolve all connection with Great Britain" was that of the Presbyterians, the Westmoreland County resolutions and the Mecklenburg Declaration; the fact that Witherspoon, a Presbyterian of the most authentic type, represented in the Continental Congress the compact Presbyterianism of the land, and that (besides his other numerous and exceedingly important services) he threw the whole weight of his own personal influence and that of those he represented, first in favor of the Declaration of Independence and then in favor of the organization of the States into a confederate union—and we have some of the grounds upon which to base an estimate of the share which Presbyterians had in building and launching that national vessel that now rides so proudly upon the billows with forty millions of voyagers on board.

# 11

# Monument to John Witherspoon

If God bade his Israel to take stones from the river's bed and build them into a monument of the Jordan passage, will he look with disfavor upon us if we gather some stones from the bed of our national Jordan, and taking some of the brass we dig from our hills shape it into the form and features of the devout, devoted, patriotic Witherspoon, and set up that figure upon those stones before the eyes of men, there to stand through coming generations, a mute but eloquent witness of what God did in those early days of heroism and trial for our beloved country though his agency and that of those he represented?

1. Such a monument will stand as an appropriate indication of the existence, claims and services of religion in our country. Our parks and public places abound with statues of secular worthies—statesmen, heroes, artists, poets and others—and is religion nothing that it should have no such representative among them?

The tourist abroad who visits the city of Worms in Germany, has his attention arrested by the magnificent statue of Luther, and catches anew the heroic spirit of the Reformation as he gazes at that noble form, the eyes raised to heaven, his left hand holding to his body a copy of the word of God, his right hand closed and laid firmly down upon it, and on his mute lips and determined brow the daring purpose, "I'll go to Worms though as many devils hinder as there are tiles on the roofs of the houses."

At Oxford, England, we see the marble forms of Cranmer, Ridley and Latimer standing there where their hot ashes smoked to heaven, for ever reciting with their pure pale lips the story of their burning; and what lover of the Lord Jesus as he gazes on those forms does not feel through his frame a thrill of the martyr-spirit? At Bedford the statue of Bunyan rises before us; and as we look and muse we think of his twelve years in Bedford jail, with his poor blind daughter at his knees, and seem to hear from those mute lips the recital again of the pilgrim's immortal tale. At Kidderminster we see the statue of Richard Baxter, "his uplifted hands," in the words of Dean Stanley, "calling to the unconverted, as of the seventeenth so of the nineteenth century, to turn and live, his seen and better world where 'there remaineth a rest for the people of God.'" At Edinburgh the statue of Andrew Melville recalls the heroism that both baffled the wiles and defied the threats of the bad regent Morton. At Glasgow you see the form of Knox towering over the city, and every element of manhood in you awakens to new energy as you gaze upon the form of that amongst men.

But where in the parks and public places of our republic will you find one solitary statue to a Christian hero? Is it not time that this monopoly of secularism be broken up?—that by such a statue as we propose the throngs who visit our public places be reminded that our thoughts are not wholly engrossed with life's secularities, and that the memories of those who have preached with lip and life the great salutary truths of Christ's religion have place in our memories and in our hearts?

2. Such a monument will symbolize the inseparable union between religion and freedom.

Witherspoon was at once an ardent Christian and an ardent patriot, and his principles of civil freedom he derived from his religion.

Have mercy on me, O Lord! I crave nothing for mine own merit, but for thy name's sake, that it may be hallowed, and for thy dear Son's sake.

Cranmer

Ridley

O Heavenly Father, I give unto thee most hearty thanks thou hast called me to profess thee unto death. Lord God, take mercy on this realm of England, and deliver the same from all her enemies.

Be of good comfort, master Ridley, and play the man, we shall this day light such a candle in England, as I trust shall never be put out.

Latimer

Indeed, no feature of our whole Revolutionary movement was more prominent than its religious spirit. The great body of the colonists were exiles for conscience' sake. Almost invariably, when the earlier public meetings were called, they were opened with prayer. Almost without exception the pastors of the people were among the most forward and most eloquent champions of the cause.

Of these men, Jonathan Mayhew, of Boston, may stand as the type. As early as 1750 we find him preaching resistance to "the first small beginnings of civil tyranny, lest it should swell to a torrent and deluge empires." Of like spirit was the eloquent Samuel Cooper, pastor of the Brattle Street church, in Boston. When the freeman "on the rivers Watauga and Holstein," in Tennessee, met together, as early as the opening of 1775, they appointed their pastor, Rev. Charles Cummings, as chairman of their committee, who expressed his own spirit and theirs in the words, "We are deliberately and resolutely determined never to surrender any of our inestimable privileges but at the expense of our lives."

On this point we cite also the following from the pen of well-known writer J. T. Headley, published recently in the *New York Observer*:

"The approaching Centennial has suddenly awakened attention to our early struggle for independence. It cannot but have a salutary effect to recall the scenes and events of that time, and to compare its leaders and statesmen with those who control our political destinies to-day, and may, perhaps, lead to a new political departure. But if the pulpit and clergy of that period do not have a large place in the imposing ceremonials proposed to be inaugurated, it will but half fulfill its true object and teach but half the lesson a true history of the Revolution rested on the pulpit. It almost trained the people in the knowledge of their political rights and made the cause of freedom the cause of God. This is seen in the fact that the Massachusetts House of Representatives passed a resolution requesting the clergy of the colony to preach on weekdays on political subjects. One can trace in the annual election-sermons, as they were called, the progress of the popular feeling. These were preached every spring before the House of Delegates on the election of a council to His Majesty's governor of the colony, and always took up the question of political rights, and discussed ably the doctrine of human freedom and the reciprocal duties and obligations of the governed and their rulers. They were afterward printed in a pamphlet form and scattered broadcast over the land. It must be remembered that there were scarcely any newspapers at that time, and the pulpit and the clergy were almost the only channels of communication between the civil authority and the people. England saw with alarm the tremendous power the clergy wielded in the colonies, and declared that they were at the bottom of the rebellion. In 1774 the governor of Massachusetts refused the request of the assembly to appoint a public fast, giving the reason 'that the request was simply to give an opportunity for sedition to flow from the pulpit.'

"Take these election-sermons from 1770 to 1775, and you can see the footprints of the rebellion. At first dealing with general principles, they, as the oppressions of the mother-country increased, applied them to the existing state of things, till the governor became alarmed at the outspoken truths he was compelled to listen to. Thus, in the spring after the tea had been thrown overboard, while Boston was still rocking like a vessel in a storm under the popular excitement, Hitchcock, a thorough Cromwellian, was selected to preach the election-sermon. Rising in his place in the House of Representatives, he thundered in the ears of the astonished governor, 'When the wicked bear rule, the people mourn.' In that discourse the governor saw clearly the indications of the coming storm. The clergy were actually in advance of the civil authorities in their views. In 1776, after the meeting of the first Continental Congress, William Godwin preaches the election-sermon, and took his text from Jeremiah xxx. 20, 21: 'Their children shall be as aforetime, and their congregation shall be established before me, and I will punish all that would oppress them, and their nobles shall be of themselves.' After reading thus far, he paused a moment, and looking over the assembled members said in an altered tone, 'The sentence is not perfected without the addition, *And the government shall proceed from the midst of them;* but the wisdom of the Continental Congress, in which we cheerfully confide, has restrained me from making it a part of my text. In an abler hand, at some fitter time, it may of itself alone *suffice for a complete text. Amen: so let it be.'* It is clear where *he* stands. He is more than ready for the Declaration of Independence. Let it come; and when it does, it will be thundered from every New England pulpit and startle every hearer like the blast of a bugle.

"But not only did the Revolution in New England rest on the shoulders of the clergy and the pulpit become the great recruiting station for the army, but a clergyman caused the first blow to be struck that has made Lexington immortal. It was on the village green, in front of Lexington Church, of which Jonas Clark was pastor, that the first blood was shed and flowed from the veins of his own parishioners. Settled on a little farm, with a salary of eighty pounds a year and twenty cords of wood, he seemed destined to exert little influence outside of his small parish; yet he started a movement that rent a kingdom asunder and is destined to revolutionize the civilized world. His wife was the cousin of John Hancock, and the two men spent many an hour discussing the great principles of human freedom and the rights of the colonies. The fruit of these discussions was given to his people from the pulpit and at the town-meetings. They, in turn, had these views embodied in instructions to their delegate to the provincial Legislature as expressing their wishes and determinations, and they remain to this day on the town records as model papers. Mr. Everett once said: 'They had no superiors and few equals.' He says, moreover: 'Mr. Clark was of a class of citizens who rendered service second to no others in enlightening and animating the popular mind on the great question at issue. I mean the patriotic clergy of New England.'

"Rev. William Ware said: 'There was no person at that time, in that vicinity—not only no clergyman, but *no* person of *whatever* calling or profession—who took a *firmer stand* for the liberties of his country.' In fact, he educated his people up to the point of resistance, and on that memorable morning of the 19$^{th}$ of April, when at two o'clock in the fierce clang of his own church-bell called his parishioners to the spot, they found their pastor already there to rouse their courage by his presence and appeals. The roll was called, and a hundred and fifth men answered to their names. What an impressive scene they presented, the pastor and his congregation, standing there in the dim starlight, under the shadow of that silent church, waiting for the clock of destiny to strike the hour! As the pastor passed along the ranks every eye gleamed with more heroic fire, and every hand grasped the firelock with a firmer clutch. Clark had trained them for that hour. 'Would they fight?' Hancock and Adams had asked. 'Yes,' said Clark; 'not only would they fight, but die right there, under the shadow of the house of God, and in the presence of their pastor.' Afterward, in the sharp rattle of musketry that followed the order, 'Throw down your arms and disperse,' Mr. Clark heard what he knew would be the result of his own teachings. When the smoke cleared away and the British had retreated, he walked up and gazed long and silently on the seven stalwart men (his own parishioners) that lay stark and stiff in death. But he shed no tears, uttered no regrets. He only murmured in solemn tones, *'From this day will be dated the liberty of the world.'* His prophetic eye saw clearly 'beyond that days' business.' And so, as we stated before, *'the teachings of the pulpit of Lexington caused the first blow to be struck for American independence.'"*

That the religious sentiment of the colonists should have been on the side of freedom was perfectly natural. For the doctrines of true religion come from the Bible, and it is there that the statesman learns that "all men are created equal, and they are endowed by their Creator with certain inalienable rights." The true equality of men was first practically exhibited when rich and poor, master and slave, male and female, sat down together at the same communion-table to eat of the same loaf and drink from the same cup. And all the sanctions of eternity are given to the doctrines of man's equality in the offer of the same heaven on precisely the same terms to prince and peasant, ignorant and enlightened. Further still, to the continued enjoyment of liberty a high degree of virtue is absolutely essential, and this virtue draws its life-blood from the religion of the word of God.

Atheism prates of human rights, and we admit that an atheist has the same rights as he who recognizes and worships the God of heaven. But we affirm that *on his own principles* he has no rights that any one is bound to respect. I have certain inalienable rights *because I am made in the image of my God,* and who touches me touches God's image. I have certain inalienable rights *because my Creator gave them to me,* and who robs me robs Jehovah. But that atheist, who "untenants creation of its God," has by his creed abolished the only source of human rights. He is the product of blind, brutish, physical forces. His body and soul are the result of a fortuitous concourse of material atoms, and as such being what *rights* can be his other than such as belong to the tree on the mountain's side against the avalanche that grinds it to powder? On the atheistic and infidel theory the only conceivable right is that which *might* bestows. The right is with the strongest.

Let infidelity and materialistic atheism prevail in our republic, destroying the very foundations of human rights, liberating the human mind from the restraints of conscience and from all sense of obligation, all awe of God and all fear of future retribution, and republican liberty and government perish for ever.

Now, in a day when a materialistic infidelity and atheism are floating in the air, breathing from the pages of magazine and newspaper, and even creeping into our schoolbooks, is it unwise, is it not at once a privilege and duty, to take this idea and put it into the bronze, and set it up where millions of eyes may see it? *The God of the Bible the only source, and the religion of the Bible the only conservator, of our inalienable rights.* Religion and liberty for ever inseparable.

3. Then the success of our Revolutionary struggle was due to the favor of God in answer to prayer.

Is it not well to set up before men the figure of him who, in addition to his other services, was ever the mover in Congress for the appointment of these repeated days of fasting, humiliation and prayer which wrought so powerfully with the people to blend piety with patriotism, and to hallow all that was dear to love of country with all that was sacred in religion?

4. Such a monument will challenge the attention of our sons and daughters to the nature and historic glories of our cherished Presbyterian system, and to the style of character which it and the body of doctrine with which it is almost invariably allied tends to create.

It is in great measure through lack of information on these points that some of them exchange their church for another as readily as they throw away an old shoestring. And it is a sign of the hour—

> God, give us men! A time like this demands
> Strong minds, great hearts, true faith and ready hands;
> Men whom the lust of office does not kill;
> Men whom the spoils of office cannot buy;

Men who possess opinions and a will;
Men who have honor; men who will not lie.

And not only men, but women too! And a little familiarity with the records of the past will people the recollection with images of stalwart men and heroic women molded and given to the world by Calvinistic Presbyterianism.

No less truthfully than eloquently does the historian Froude write of Calvinism that it has "inspired and sustained the bravest efforts ever made by man to break the yoke of unjust authority."

"When all else has failed, when patriotism has covered its face and human courage has broken down, when intellect has yielded, as Gibbon says, with a 'smile or a sigh,' content to philosophize in the closet and abroad worship with the vulgar, when emotion and sentiment and tender, imaginative piety have become the handmaids of superstition, and have dreamed themselves into forgetfulness that there is any difference between lies and truth—the slavish form of belief called Calvinism, in one or other of its many forms, has borne ever an inflexible front to illusion and mendacity, and has preferred rather to be ground to powder like flint than to bend before violence or melt under enervating temptation."

FROUDE

CALVINISM INSPIRED AND SUSTAINED THE BRAVEST EFFORTS EVER MADE BY MAN TO BREAK THE YOKE OF UNJUST AUTHORITY.

Our youth need to be taught, and peradventure some of their elders reminded, that Coligny and his noble army of French Huguenots were to a man Calvinistic Presbyterians—that William the Silent and his Dutch heroes, who bore so heroically the long agony of Spanish oppression, and at last chased the cruel minions of Philip and the pope out of the Netherlands and built a republic on the ruins of despotism, were Calvinistic Presbyterians.

What style of womanhood comes from the hands of Calvinistic Presbyterianism we may see in the person of Colgny's wife, the noble *Charlotte de Laval.* The admiral, wounded and taken prisoner at the memorable battle of St. Quentin, had been conveyed to Ghent. During his sickness and imprisonment there his hand fell upon a copy of the word of God. As he read and mused he was led by the Spirit of God to accept salvation as offered in the gospel. Sitting one evening after his liberation and return to Chatillon upon a balcony of the castle, and at his side Charlotte his wife, who "was wonderfully given to the Reformed religion," they looking together at the silver stars, she said to him:

"How wonderful that you and your brother Andelot should have been blest in your captivity with a knowledge of the truth! And why do you not now publicly avow your faith as he has done?"

"Sound your soul, he answered. "Are you prepared to hear of defection, to receive the reproaches of partisans as well as enemies, treasons of your friends, exile, shame, nakedness, hunger, even the hunger of your own children, your own death by an executioner, after that of your husband? I have you three weeks to consider."

"They are gone already," replied his wife. "Do not bring upon your head the deaths of those three weeks, or I will myself bear witness against you at the judgment-seat of God."

"Enough, madame," said he. "It was only for your sake that I thought of these terrors."

At once he professed himself a follower of the Reformation. And on St. Bartholomew's bloody eve they stabbed him to death in his own chamber and threw his body out of the window, cut off his venerable head and set it, a choice and welcome present, to the pope, and for three days the abjects of Paris dragged the lifeless trunk through the streets, and hung it up by the heels upon the gibbet.

See, too, the heroic wife of John Welsh begging of England's coarse, cruel king the favor that her poor sick husband, fourteen years in exile and pining for a breath of his native air, might return to his home.

"Whose daughter are you?" James demanded.

"The daughter of John Knox."

"Knox and Welsh! The devil never made such a match as that."

"Very like, Your Majesty; we never asked his advice.

"What children did your father leave?"

"Three, Your Majesty."

"Were they lads or lasses?"

"Lasses, Your Majesty."

"The Lord be praised! Had they been lads, I could not have kept my seat upon my throne."

Witherspoon was one of those banes of a later generation, and King George was not able to keep seat on the American portion of his throne.

"But give him his native air, sir," begged the woman.

"Give him the devil! Answered the brutal king.

"Give that, sir, to your hungry courtiers."

"Well, he may return if he will conform."

Lifting her apron, she answered, "I would rather take his head here."

And need we speak of Knox, whom Carlyle pronounced "the bravest of all Scotchmen," whom Froude calls "the representative of all that was best in Scotland," and of whom he adds, "no grander figure can be found in the history of the Reformation in this island?"

It was quite in the course of things that Witherspoon should plead so earnestly in behalf of the Declaration, for the chief sentiment of that immortal paper had been announced by Knox, his great ancestor, two hundred years before. It was in the presence of the beautiful but wicked Mary queen of Scots.

"Think you," asked the queen, with indignant amazement—"think you that subjects, having the power, may resist their princes?"

To which Knox replied: "If princes exceed their bounds, madam, no doubt they may be resisted even by power. For no greater honor or greater obedience is to be given to princes than God has ordained to be given to father and mother. But the father may be struck with a frenzy in which he would slay for his children. Now, madam, if the children arise, join together, apprehend the father, take the sword from him, bind his hands and keep him in prison till the frenzy

THE BRAVEST OF ALL SCOTCHMEN...

...THE REPRESENTATIVE OF ALL THAT WAS BEST IN SCOTLAND...

...NO GRANDER FIGURE CAN BE FOUND IN THE HISTORY OF THE REFORMATION IN THIS ISLAND.

JOHN KNOX

be over, think you, madam, that the children do any wrong? Even so, madam, it is with princes that would murder the children of God that are subject unto them. Their blind zeal is nothing but a mad frenzy; therefore, to take the sword from them, to bind their hands and to cast them into prison till they be brought to a more sober mind is no disobedience against princes, but true obedience, because it agreeth with the will of God."

"Thus spoke Calvinism," writes Froude, "the creed of republics."

And Andrew Melville.

The bad regent Morton, scowling and biting the head of his staff, growled: "There will never be quietness in this country till half a dozen of you be hanged or banished."

"Tush, sir!" answered Melville; "Threaten your courtiers after this manner. It is the same to me whether I rot in the air or under the ground. I have been ready to give my life where it would not be half so well expended."

And those brave Covenanters who spread their declaration of independence on the broad tombstone in Gray Friars' churchyard, and signed it, some of them, with a pen dipped in their veins, opened for the purpose. This covenant in its remotest consequences took off the head of Charles I of Wentworth and Laud, the three great tyrants who had bound England, Church and State, hand and foot like a very slave, and thus liberated England and saved constitutional liberty for the world.

This is the sort of character that Calvinistic Presbyterianism has given to the world. Would our society be any the worse for a few more like them? Would it harm our sons and daughters to receive a new endowment of this style of moral nerve and muscle?

5. Such a monument will be a ceaseless iteration of the fact that to a very large degree the seed whose fruit we, as citizens of this republic, are now harvesting, in our principles of civil and religious

freedom, in our intelligence and means of culture and in the nations' marvelous march to greatness, was sown by Presbyterian hands.

Finally, the unveiling of this statue during the Centennial period, with prayer and praise and oration, will call the attention of the nation and the world to these facts, reminding them that the Presbyterian Church is, in its nature and form, a representative republic, and that, ever hated by tyrants, ever a champion of truths that create moral nerve and muscle and fit met to dare and do an endure, it has deserved, and does deserve, a deep place in the gratitude and a high place in the admiration of the nation for its services in the cause of God and man.

THE END

LaVergne, TN USA
17 December 2009

167377LV00002B/1/P

9 780915 815302